Y0-CCU-196

S.C. 818.54 INKP Copy 3

Inkplots

South Carolina State Library
Columbia, S.C.

INKPLOTS

INKPLOTS

Random Acts of Writing

The Inkplots
Writers Group

22-MORT

Copyright © 1998 by The Inkplots Writers Group.

Cover Art : "Reading Under Moonlight"
Used with the gracious permission of Jelene Morris.

Library of Congress Number: 98-89495
ISBN#:   Hardcover   0-7388-0257-3
                Softcover   0-7388-0258-1

All rights reserved. No part of this book may be reproduced or transmitted in
any form or by any means, electronic or mechanical, including photocopying,
recording, or by any information storage and retrieval system, without permission
in writing from the copyright owner.

This is a work of fiction. Names, characters, places and incidents either are the
product of the author's imagination or are used fictitiously, and any resemblance
to any actual persons, living or dead, events, or locales is entirely coincidental.

This book was printed in the United States of America.

To order additional copies of this book, contact:
Xlibris Corporation   1-888-7-XLIBRIS
PO Box 2199   1-609-278-0075
Princeton, NJ 08543-2199   www.Xlibris.com
USA   Orders@Xlibris.com

CONTENTS

INTRODUCTION

Welcome to the collected musings of the Inkplots. Before you turn another page, you should know that you are about to embark on the adventures of ten eclectic and disparate writers—two members of the legal profession, two mental health professionals, a corporate communications veteran, an artist, a librarian, a coliseum director, a retiree, and a professional wrestler. Together we comprise a writers group called the Inkplots.

Southerners all, we both define and defy the mysterious genre of "Southern writing." Our work is inexorably tied to time and place, whether set in the mill villages of Spartanburg, South Carolina in 1958 or an Austrian concentration camp during World War II. Our voices speak to the human experience—its magnificent triumphs and its heart wrenching tragedies.

We all share a love of the language, its incongruous marriage of precision and marvelous ambiguity. Through the medium of words we paint slice-of-life portraits using our readers' imaginations as canvases. The beauty of the written word is that our protagonists will look, sound, feel, and smell differently to each reader—our words a delicately choreographed interpretive dance with you as the sole judge of a character's vibrancy and meaning.

We also share a love of writing. We are the storytellers who pass on tales of the extraordinary amidst the mundane, who find humor in the most unlikely places, and who memorialize it in writing for anyone who chooses to read it.

We hope you enjoy these works. A writer's only audience, after all, is a reader. Now, please begin your journey to our worlds. *Bon voyage*.

—*The Authors*

EXTRACT FROM
HER OWN LAW[1]

A Novel by C. Tolbert Goolsby, Jr.

Another man what come by to pay his respects, Skeets said, was Lindel Carmichael, a man what once worked for Mr. Cumbee when him and his brother owned a cotton gin over in Calhoun County and before Mr. Cumbee met up with Skeets's aunt. Skeets said when Lindel come to the house, he had on about the tightest white suit he'd ever seen on a grown man. Skeets said it was so tight on him his cheeks was all puffed out and his eyes, they was bulging and looked like they was on stems.

Skeets said he watched Lindel stand at Mr. Cumbee's coffin for a few minutes and then seen him go over to his aunt and tell her how sorry he was and all about the unfortunate accident what killed Mr. Cumbee. After he got through doing that, Skeets said him and Lindel, they come in the parlor to get theirself a glass of ice cold tea to drink. There was a few old ladies from the missionary society setting around in the parlor and they was talking about what'd happened to Mr. Cumbee and about how awful it was and everything and wondering what in the world his aunt was gonna do now that Mr. Cumbee was dead and gone.

That's when, Skeets said, Lindel seen this here cane bottom chair over near the fireplace. Nobody'd set down on it because it had a big old hole right in the middle of it. But Lindel, he didn't seem to care none or he didn't see the hole one, cause he set hisself down on it.

Wellsir, Lindel's suit, it was so tight on him that when he set down on the chair Skeets said the seat of Lindel's britches split right slap in two. When that happened, Skeets seen Lindel's jewels fall down outta his britches and through the hole what was in the chair. Skeets said even though Lindel musta felt it when his pants split wide open and his jewels fell out, he just set there and acted like there wasn't nothing wrong. Skeets told me the way he figured it at the time was Lindel musta felt like he couldn't do nothing else right then on account of them old ladies still being there in the room with them. Anyhow, Skeets said about that time this here tom cat come in the room and when it seen Lindel's jewels hanging there, it run over and got under the chair and started slapping at them with its front paws. The cat, Skeets said, slapped at Lindel's jewels first with its left paw and then with its right one, making them swing right and left, back and forth, back and forth. Skeets said it reminded him of a boxer hitting at a boxing bag.

After while, Skeets said he seen Lindel try to stand up a little to try and get away from the cat. He said whenever Lindel raised up outta the chair, the cat grabbed hold to Lindel's jewels with both its front paws and held on as tight and as hard as it could.

Before Skeets could do anything to help Lindel out, he said his aunt walked in the parlor and seen the cat playing under the chair with Lindel's jewels. She went over to the fireplace and picked up these here tongs and bent down by the chair Lindel was setting in and told the cat to scat, which it done. Then, she reached under the chair with the tongs, saying something or other about the cat getting an old furball all hung up in the bottom of the chair. The next thing she done, Skeets said, was to grab hold to Lindel's jewels with the tongs. She was just about ready to give them a good yank, when Lindel, Skeets said, let go with a scream what folks could hear all the way up to Atlanta, Georgia. Skeets said, when his aunt heard the scream, she looked and seen what she was doing and let loose the tongs.

Old Lindel, he jumped up outta his chair and took off running, Skeets said, with the cat chasing right behind him. Skeets

said ain't nobody seen hide nor hair of Lindel since. The cat neither. All his aunt ever said about it, Skeets said, was she wondered
what kind of damn pervert that was? When the lady she was talking to said she didn't think Lindel was no pervert, his aunt said, "I
ain't talking about Lindel. I'm talking about that stupid cat."

MORT

RENEWAL

A beautiful quilt, lovingly patched, delicately stitched in expand-
  ing rows, spaced closely.
Softness that comes from years of warming and comforting, en-
  abling bits and pieces to edge into needed spots.
A rent that appears as a pinprick, expanded to a gash by a foot in sleep.
A silent invisible nibbles at the edges,
Dots of the cotton soul are scattered and lost,
Shreds where binding once held tight,
A gaping ragged emptiness at its center, oozing,
Fading reds and blues, no longer able to comfort,
Cast into a corner too late for a needle's help.
Rediscovered by another who can feel the warmth and comfort in
  the ragged softness.
Snipped and stitched into another shape,
Delicately mended, patched and changed,
Reborn.

—Ann Furr

WHY I SELDOM WRITE LONG POEMS

"If you need all those words,"
my father, the photographer,
once told me, "then write an essay."
He traveled with one
Speed Graphic in the
old days and "Click Zoop"
which had a Zeiss lens
and was retrieved from
a German airplane
shot down over France.
Unlike his counterparts
who traveled with an
entourage of metal cases,
he had one modest
case of clips and was
known for economy
of motion and product
responses to The Company
as they tried to perfect
color film in every light.
He Mastered Photography
in the darkroom,
with a minimum of negatives
and expected his daughter to
do no less with words.

—*Righton H. McCallum*

MORT

A DRINKING WOMAN

Carla Damron

"A vodka tonic, please," I say to the pretty woman in the short black skirt. I hope I sound like a woman who belonged there, like someone biding my time before an important meeting or a romantic evening out. As the waitress wanders off, I hear the click of her high, shiny black shoes on the wood floor and I wonder how she moves so efficiently on her tiptoes. I sit up straight in my chair and await her return with my drink.

These are the hardest moments. I am so fiercely alone. All around me, I feel eyes glaring at me with disapproval. When I was young, I thought I could be invisible. I could close my eyes and disappear into a world as quiet as a still, moonless night.

But I am not invisible now.

My eyes shift around the room, studying the other patrons in the bar. I see a man alone in the corner who has loosened his necktie and rolled up his sleeves. His hand looks solid as granite holding his drink.

I am reminded of my father's strong hand around his very favorite glass. I can see him coming home from work, throwing his suit jacket on a chair and reaching under the sink for the vodka he'd pour into the squat green tumbler. I hear the clink of the ice as he slapped the drained glass on to the table. It never stayed empty very long.

"Dance with me," my father would say.

I am five years old, and I reach for his outstretched hand. My tiptoes rest on the tops of his giant shoes, my head tilts up to look in his laughing eyes. Andy Williams sings "Try to Remember" on our record player as my father twirls me around and my giggles make him smile. But we cannot dance for very long. He will reach for the glass again and again and soon, he is unsteady as a toddler on his feet. I want him to swing me around again but he yells at me. Don't I know how tired he is? How fed up he is?

And I'd close my eyes and disappear once again.

Now a tall woman enters the bar. Her walk is quick and purposeful, her blue dress falls like water over her thin, graceful body. She scans the room with her large eyes that pass by me so quickly that I think maybe I am invisible.

She spots the man in the corner and waves three fluttering fingers at him as she approaches. His right hand lets go of his beer as he stands, embraces her, and kisses her softly on the cheek. She rakes her hand through her long dark hair and lets it fly behind her before she eases into the chair beside him.

The waitress takes her order before she comes to my table with my drink, which I sip nervously. It is cold on my teeth but sends a burn into my nostrils. The bitter taste quickly passes as it sizzles down my throat. I close my eyes, hoping no one notices my school-girl discomfort.

I glance at the other woman. She whispers to the man and lowers her eyes. He touches her, her gaze lifts up to his face again and he smiles at her. I can tell he knows her— knows the darkest, most hidden corners of her because she lets him in. She is un-ashamed.

I feel dizzy now. My breath coming into my lungs is leaden. I want to disappear into that place as dark and private as the moon-less night.

I think of my mother. When she was young, she had been as beautiful as that woman. Her blond hair fell in soft waves off her shoulders and her ready smile could intoxicate any lover. My father claimed her as a prize on their wedding day and loved her so completely that when I came, one year later, he felt he'd lost her. I was a sickly, loud infant, he often told me. Why did I cry so much? Why couldn't I be comforted?

The waitress brings the woman some wine. She lifts the glass by the stem, her nails are crimson points on long, elegant fingers. Wispy bangs brush her delicate brows. I imagine her scent, a breath of flowers that he inhales. Her eyes are wide, dark pools fixed on him, drinking in his every word, his every expression. He leans into her and whispers something that makes her laugh. He kisses her. Her mouth against his is still laughing, and he smiles as he pulls back, whispers again, and then touches her soft, flushed cheek.

I lift my glass, studying my gnawed fingernails as they grip the tumbler. I take a quick gulp. And another. My chest feels warm. A strange tingling spreads to my fingers and the top of my head. I inhale deeply, the breath going out of me trips over itself. One more sip.

She holds the wine close to the candle on their table. The claret color glows like her lips, which pull back in a half-moon smile. She turns to face him. Neither speaks. They are beyond words as their eyes hold each other.

I imagine I have a lover, too. He is tall and strong, with a dimpled smile and thick dark hair. He holds me with his eyes and kisses my lips and strokes my cheek. I would lean into him and whisper soft words that make him smile, make him fill up with me.

And I don't want to be invisible.

I'm aware that my eyes are closed and I pray no one is watching me. My lids open and I stare into the clear mirror surface of my drink. Mirrors were never my friends. As young as middle school, I dreaded the most fleeting glance of my own reflection. A plump, shapeless body, a nose too long. My hair hanging like dead sea weed. The thin lips that made up my crooked smile.

"Cover your mouth," my mother had said. "Your smile is not your best feature." The woman takes the man's hand and they rise from the table. His arm around her waist makes her feel safe and loved. She tilts her head against his shoulder as they slowly head towards the door.

My trembling hand reaches for my glass again. I lift it to my mouth, empty it in four quick swallows, and then I sigh.

"Another vodka tonic, please," I say to the waitress.

BENCH MADE

This?
That?
Just?
Fair?
Old?
New?
Who?
Why?
How?
When?
Where?
We Agree or We Disagree
Affirmed, Reversed, or Vacated
Dismissed, Quashed, or Remanded
Motion Granted or Motion Denied
Petition Granted or Petition Denied
Appeal, Certiorari, or Mandamus
Quo Warranto or Habeas Corpus
I Concur, I Dissent

—Bert Goolsby

MOTHER TONGUE

I knew a tongue once
lashed around people's bodies
ate its own children, spewed
hatred, spawned violence
and finally choked its
owner to death by
coiling like a rattlesnake
around her epiglottis.
But, that's not
the end of the story.
Even her tombstone
tilted after several years
and cracked when ice
collected in its words,
mute testament to a
vitriolic life.
Her family chose not
to replace it.

—*Righton H. McCallum*

TRIBAL HEIRLOOM

Judy Hubbard

Thrift stores lay strung like Christmas tree lights along Two Notch Road as it wound through Columbia, South Carolina. Lined with run-down retail stores, this thoroughfare carried heavy traffic and served as a footpath for our local prostitutes. I made a weekly circuit of five stores and never came home empty-handed. My personal favorite, the Community Thrift, stocked the most extensive and best organized selections. Low but firm prices and rapid turnover of inventory compelled me to return each week.

There I experienced moments of pure bargain hunting joy—a soft inviting sofa for twenty dollars, an arguably art deco lamp for ninety-five cents, a Catawba-like black pottery vessel, curious oil paintings, funky 1950s kitchenware, handmade pieced quilts and linens—all priced for a few dollars. It was a place of infinite, affordable possibilities.

Most thrift stores come in plain packages. The Community Thrift occupied a faded yellow "Butler" building fronted by a parking lot jammed with everything from rusting Oldsmobiles to shiny BMWs and suburban minivans. Testy spouses and bored children waited impatiently in the parked vehicles, doors propped open, while serious pursuits went on inside.

Shoppers came from one of three hunting "tribes." The Tribe of Necessity bought clothes, toys and practical household goods. The Tribe of Boredom hunted whimsical bric-a-brac and festive clothing. The Tribe of Collectors sought older, more valuable prey, like dolls, imported china and pedigreed furniture.

I belonged to this last tribe, honing my hunter-gatherer skills from an early age. At five, I searched broad white sand beaches for perfect seashells; the back of my small neck would glow bright red indicating the relentless nature of my pursuit.

We "Collectors" knew each other, not by name, but by what could be observed in brief thrift shopping encounters. He-Who-Likes-Golf-Clubs, She-Who-Gathers-Aluminum, Mother-with-Jumping-Boy, Lady-with-Big-Earrings all stalked the hunting grounds with me.

My passion and my dollars succumbed easily to sensuous textures, patina-rich surfaces, narrative content and reconfigurative potential. The name She-Who-Buys-A-Lot described so many of my tribe that the simple name Blue-Van-Woman more accurately evoked my place in the tribe.

Competitive collecting demanded spontaneous decisions so Collectors all drove big vehicles—station wagons or vans. Few finds could not be coaxed into the cargo space of my metallic iris-blue Chrysler Town and Country minivan.

The people of my tribe cut swift, quiet hunting trails through thrift store aisles, stalking down the one worthy find among the thousand pieces that threatened distraction. The tribesmen of Necessity and Boredom socialized as they shopped, but my kinsmen never spoke unless forced to linger in the check-out line. The Collectors focused totally on the stalking.

Every tribe has its hunting legends of great pursuits, noble prey and dangerous capture. Told again and again, these legends preserve tribal legacy and point the way for those who would follow.

On a spring-like late winter's day, I, Blue-Van-Woman, set out on my usual hunt, no more than twenty dollars in my small hunting bag.

I saw the table almost as soon as I entered. Made of mahogany the color of ginger cookies, the gracious but restrained Hepplewhite style could extend to accomodate eight people. The drop leaf sides looked like big swooping wings hanging down so they nearly touched the floor. Slender legs tapered fluidly to simple square tips. This magnificent table had all the characteristics of a fine racehorse: color, line, pedigree.

Alive with the passion of the hunt, I moved nimbly to be the first of my tribe to claim the prize. But, drawing near, the crudely written sticker declared the impossible price: four hundred and ninety-nine dollars. I moaned with disappointment.

As the weeks and then months passed, I continued my regular circuit of the thrift stores. Like the wise eight-point buck that eludes hunters and their guns, the table remained unclaimed, uncaptured as it stood in exactly the same spot by the front door. In thrift store time, months counted as years.

Each time I came to "hunt" the Community Thrift I would take a moment to commune with the noble table. My eyes scanned the price sticker while the tips of my fingers lingered on the broad mahogany surface. Occasionally, I would lift one of the drop leaves just to appreciate its ample proportions.

Would it have fixed so strongly in my mind had it been in a proper place, like an antique store?

One day I noticed that the price had been reduced to three hundred and ninety-nine dollars, and I felt almost embarassed for the table. Then, weeks later the price dropped again, this time to two hundred and ninety-nine dollars. My instincts sharpened and I took aim once again at the quarry.

As a Collector, I had learned well the skills of rationalizing purchases. Still, two hundred and ninety-nine dollars exceeded justification, and I resisted the taking. The table remained in the forest of the thrift world.

Another day, weeks later, I came again to the Community Thrift.

"Could this really be right?" I thought and reread the numerals marking the table. Scratched through again and now again, the table's price sticker read an irresistible one hundred and ninety-nine dollars.

The stalking ended. The next stage of the hunt commenced—negotiation.

Boldly, I pulled the table free from the crowded herd of furniture. Like a lanky adolescent stretching after a long car ride, the table extended as I opened its vast leaves. I could almost hear the sigh of relief as it expanded. Its length and breadth overwhelmed me.

I knew this table could be a fine legacy, and I began to imagine how this noble table was a stage upon which yet-to-be-written scenes would be played out.

My husband and I already owned a massive round Victorian table that could extend to seat twenty people, and our sons battled over who would inherit it. Could this table resolve their conflict?

My mother had asked me to find a special present for Will, my younger son, to celebrate his college graduation. In my mind's eye I could imagine Will, his friends, and his family eating and conversing around it. Even this reduced thrift store price slightly exceeded Mother's budget, but what a magnificent present it would be.

Something about the table caught my eye and reined in my musings. The noble table had been wounded. Scratched into the table's main surface, the letters "F-U-C-K" now marred the mahogany plane.

Surely a clever person like myself could heal such a wound. Reclamation and restoration were my specialties. Surely, I could make this table whole and well-mannered again. Who would want a table that insulted at every meal? At one time, this had been a high-class table, but right now it spoke guttertalk.

From across the store, the blond female manager saw me examining the table. She came over and spoke, and we began a cautious tango of negotiation. She was young and tough, while I kept my tribal wisdom hidden behind a sweet smile as I pointed out the disfiguring marks. The table had been there for a long time and she could read the graffiti, as well as my interest. So, perhaps to remove it from any further harm, in this place that never negotiated prices, she did—one hundred and fifty dollars.

I sealed the agreement, and blue-vanned to the bank for the cash, the only acceptable thrift store method of payment. With victory and satisfaction, I loaded the table into my roomy vehicle and carried it home.

Few would prize a table that said "F-U-C-K." That my refined Baptist mother would give such a table confounded the mind. This would not be the sort of legacy she would wish to pass on and I had been duplicitous to buy it with this knowledge. She would love to give this table, but she would never have bought a table so mutilated. Luckily, Mother lived out-of-state.

Never did I doubt that I could reclaim propriety for the table, my mother and my son. I had performed similar feats of reclaimation before. Surely, I could do this. Surely.

Once home, I assembled the tools of transformation—fine steel wool, Old English Scratch Cover, soft rags and furniture polish. (My tribe always had such paraphernalia close at hand.) With absolute confidence, I began my magic.

A fine steel wool buffing…"F-U-C-K"

Again and again…still, "F-U-C-K"

Not so fine steel wool buffing…"F-U-C-K"

Heavy buffing…"F-U-C-K"

Old English Scratch Cover…"F-U-C-K"

I began to worry. Surely, I could erase this.

More scratch cover…"F-U-C-K"

Heavy application of scratch cover over the whole table surface…"F-U-C-K"

Paste wax and buffing…"F-U-C-K"

My magic began to teeter and slip.

Indeed, the more polished and shiny the table surface grew, the more the word seemed to stand out.

Time and my optimism vanished.

With a solemn promise of secrecy, Will received this almost

wonderful table from his uninformed grandmother. With youthful enthusiasm, Will repeated all of my efforts and had the same results.

Misfortune upon misfortune, the vandal had carved his graffiti right on the edge of the table top where no lamp or magazine could camouflage the flaw. In the short time before Will's grad school commenced, we could not refinish the table.

I was stymied, brought low, humiliated, defeated.

Will said that he could live with the text-ridden table, but I could find no peace with it.

Josh, our older son, brought an irreverent approach. With total disregard for the nobility of the table, he quipped, "Why don't we just change 'Fuck' to 'Bucky?' At least it wouldn't be so offensive."

And there it was, the perfect solution.

I took out my carving tool and, carefully mimicking the crudeness of the unknown vandal's marks, I transformed the "F" into a "B" and added "N-E-R." It now spelled my paternal grandmother's maiden name, Buckner.

In a family that prizes family antiques and good stories, we respectfully refer to Will's graduation gift as the "Buckner Table." I wonder, how long we will say it without smiling?

THE SWINGING NECKBREAKER: A NIGHT ON THE ROAD

Sam Morton

"Try not to hurt me tonight, Bubba," Bruno said as I walked into the locker room, an amply stuffed athletic bag draped over my shoulder.

"Hurt you? You're the one they call 'The Crippler,'" I said as I laid my bag on the floor next to his. He had laced up one boot and was wrapping white athletic tape around his other ankle. The tape scrooched as he pulled it from the roll and patted down against his ankle punctuating the low din of the other boys' conversations as echoing off of cold tile walls.

Bruno and I are professional wrestlers. Not the "stylin', profilin', Lear-jet-flyin'" boys of the big leagues, but the cram-six-guys-in-a-van-and-head-to-the-high school-gym variety.

"So Bruno," I said pulling my tights on over my kneepads, precariously balancing on one foot and holding onto the back of a metal folding chair, "What's the deal tonight?"

"Tony wants you to go over. But we need to set it up so I screw myself in the finish so I can challenge you to a rematch."

"I thought we were tagging with Neal and J.D.," I said, suddenly noticing that thirty-five minutes before bell time, neither one of them there.

Bruno got a disgusted look on his face, "J.D. cancelled out. He says he's quitting the biz…again. His ol' lady's on his ass 'cause he didn't mow the lawn or fix the roof or something. So he's quit for the umpteenth time. He's so freakin' whipped, it's pitiful."

"Think he'll be at the show on the twenty-eighth?" I asked without looking up from lacing my boots.

"Hell yeah," Bruno said with confidence.

"What about Neal? We could've had a handicapped tag match and both of us whip your sorry behind from one end of the ring to the other."

"His mother-in-law died."

"Oh, man, I'm sorry to hear that," I said, feeling bad for him.

"Well, he's not. Listen to this," Bruno said, scooting his chair close and leaning his head toward mine as if about to impart a great secret. "Neal said his mother-in-law has been staying with him and his wife for the past four days. He got up yesterday and went in to her bedroom to get something and she was graveyard dead—stiff as a board and white all over with drool running out of her mouth."

"That's a hell of a way to start your day, ain't it?" I said.

"Wait, it gets better. He didn't want to be the one to upset his wife by telling her, so he eased out of the room and shut the door. The lousy SOB went down and ate breakfast like nothing was wrong. Then, after about an hour, he looked at his wife and said, 'Gee, your mom sure has been asleep a long time. Should you go check on her?'"

I thought Bruno was going to fall off his chair when he got to the end of that story. We both laughed till tears ran down our cheeks.

Both of us had been to the "big show" as people in the business call the huge television productions. The good guys—called the faces (as in baby faces)—and the bad guys—the heels, each got a dressing room equipped with a television monitor and two-way radios so opponents could talk and plan their matches. At the big show, everyone stayed busy. It was all glitz—image the commodity for sale.

But this regional circuit is different, with a more gritty and in-the-trenches feel. Here the money sucks, so the fans become our focus. The show is the thing. Though combatants in the ring, we're all great friends backstage.

Not a drop of wax ever touch the locker room floors we use on the regional circuit. They're swept clean by a high school janitor, more often than not an older black man named Joe or something similar. In the crevices and corners lie the orange-brown granules he throws out to attract the dust. To me it always looks and smells like ground-up pencil erasers.

The heels and faces share the same facility, usually a gym locker room with leaky, white porcelain plumbing fixtures. Green hard-water stains bubble up in the condensation that makes the air heavy and accumulates on the steel fixtures causing rust to streak to the floor.

Glossy white paint flakes off the cinder block walls of this school, probably built forty years ago. Above the top of one wall sits a conglomeration of small-paned windows, the kind that tilt out from the bottom. Pale sunlight leaks in through the panes encrusted with dust and grime and veined with cracks. In the sections where the glass was completely shattered out, the sun beams through in honey-toned crystal columns and flecks of lint and dust dance in the yellow light.

No, it wasn't Madison Square Garden or the Calgary Stampede, but in the intimacy of such raw conditions, I found my motivation. Amid the stale odor of gym clothes and the musty scent of mildewed tile, we came to deliver a real show to real people. No lights, no camera, but all action.

Fully dressed in our wrestling gear, Bruno and I leaned forward against the tile wall, stretching our Achilles tendons and calf muscles.

"Why don't we just call it in the ring," Bruno said. "We've

been at this long enough to make it look good."

Tony, the promoter, walked by. "You guys are third match. You're going over," he told me. "Where you wanna be from and how much do you wanna weigh?" Tony asked, a half-inch cigar stub slurring his heavily accented Jersey speech.

"I'll be from Los Angeles and make me…I dunno, 266 pounds."

"How 'bout you, Crippler?" Tony asked still scribbling my information on the back of an envelope.

"Make me 280 pounds and from wherever the hell I wanna be from. That oughta get 'em pissed off right away."

Tony drifted over to the next huddle of wrestlers to get their information. Even through the closed locker room door, I could hear the excited conversation of little children. Then the bell rang seven times, resounding throughout the cavernous gym, bouncing off all four walls and amplifying itself each time. This is it, I thought. It's show time.

Bruno had already walked to the ring and was harassing the fans when I heard my music crank up. ZZ Top's *Sharp Dressed Man* reverberated off the walls and I heard the announcer begin.

"And now, making his way to the ring, weighing in at 266 pounds, hailing from Los Angeles, California, he is Sweetness…Johnny Blitz."

The fans screamed—honest-to-God screamed, and it was the best feeling in the world. That's why I continue to do it. Why I travel from town to town in the back of a ratty van with five other guys whose socks stink. It's the one and only reason.

I climbed through the ropes.

"Kill him, Sweetness," a man yelled.

Bruno motioned for the ring announcer to hand him the microphone. "Hey! All you rednecks shut up and let me say something." A chorus of boos greeted him and a few kids shot him the bird.

He continued, "It looks like as many of you as could afford it paid to see me tonight. One things for sure, there're some empty double-wides in this town tonight." The boos got louder. "You wanted to see greatness? Well, here I am. So all you beer-guzzlin' wrestler wannabes and you fat, ugly women married to 'em, sit back and shut up and watch me take this punk to school."

That was my cue. I jumped him from behind, threw him into the ropes and cut him down with a clothesline across the throat. The crowd popped out of the seats.

He got up and I drilled him with an elbow to the jaw and then dropped an elbow across his throat as he lay on the mat. I tried for a quick pinfall, but he kicked out.

I got off the mat, grabbed him by the chin, and prepared to push him into the ropes again for another high-impact move, but he pretended to gouge my eyes. I fell to the floor, screaming and blinking my eyes uncontrollably, "selling" the move.

Bruno grasped me by my hair and pulled me into the corner. My back against the turnbuckle, he slapped me full force with the palm of his hand against my left breast with a backhanded, Indian chop. That was one move you just couldn't fake in the ring.

Sweat sprayed off my chest as if from an atomizer. I felt the tiny surface veins break and the blood spider-web out from the point of impact. The slap sounded so loud, that the crowd at once winced and let out a collective, "Ooh."

"What do you think about your Sweetness now," he yelled as he pushed my head back preparing to deliver another chop.

"Let him go you son-of-a-bitch," yelled a woman in the front row.

""This one's for you, baby doll," the Crippler replied. He slapped me again and I bent over and staggered out of the corner in mock agony. The sweat beaded on my brow from the heat of the lights. I walked on my tiptoes, shaking my left arm, pretending to wave off the numbness caused by the chops.

Bruno grabbed me by the hair again, pulling me back into the corner. He delivered a third chop, but I rebounded as if gaining momentum. I clutched the straps on the front of his tights, turned him into the corner and gave him three quick, stinging chops.

And then I pulled him by his head and flipped him into the center of the ring.

Jumping high into the air, I extended one leg and dropped it hard against Bruno's chest. I landed with a crash on the mat so hard both of us bounced nearly a foot in the air. The fans went wild, pressing against the security railing next to the ring.

"Tear his damn head off, Johnny," screamed one man, tobacco juice streaming down the corner of his cheek.

I executed a series of quick moves—a drop kick, a flying clothesline, and a splash from the top rope where I dove from four feet above Bruno and laid out across him, softening the blow by catching myself on my arms and knees. Every time he hit the mat, it sounded like the ring was going to collapse and the crowd screamed louder.

I covered him for another pin. The referee counted, "One, two…" Bruno raised his shoulder.

I doubled him over, picked him up by his waist and dropped him on his back executing a power bomb. I lay across his chest to cover him for the three-count pinfall. Count. "One, two…" He kicked out.

I stood him straight up, bounced off the rope and delivered a roundhouse kick to the side of his head, ever so slightly pulled to avoid injuring him. Cover. Count. "One, two…" He grabbed the rope, breaking the count.

I stood up chest-to-chest with the referee, "Can't you count any faster," I yelled. That was Bruno's cue. He drove his elbow right into my groin, a classic heel move when conventional wrestling fails.

I buckled my knees and fell to the mat face first. I pretended to convulse in pain. The fans threw cups and ice and popcorn boxes into the ring. Bruno smiled at them. "Which one of you toothless, illiterate hayseeds wants to be next, huh?" They cursed his mother. They threatened to kill him. It was great!

The end was near. One trip outside the ring and Bruno would screw himself, giving me the victory. I still shivered on the mat.

He placed one hand on my hair and one on the waistband of my tights. Picking me up slowly, he leaned into me placing his mouth against my ear where he could talk and no one would see.

"See the girl in the short white dress on the front row?" He asked.

"Uh huh," I grunted.

"I don't think she's wearing any panties. I think she wants me. I'm going to throw you out on that side of the ring. If you see anything good, you better tell me."

With that he thrust me through the second rope. I landed with a loud thud on the hardwood gym floor. Bruno followed me out and picked up a folding metal chair. He propped it against the ring post, intending to throw me into it. I lay motionless, face down. He picked me up, took my arm, and with as much momentum as he could muster, tried to sling me against the chair.

At the last second before he let me go, finding "miraculous" inner strength, I reversed the move and sent him reeling headfirst into the seat. His head hitting the chair sounded like I had kicked down a steel door. The fans erupted again. Slowly, nearly spent, I rolled Bruno back into the ring. Laying beside him, I barely had the strength to lay my arm over his heaving chest. Cover. Count. "One, two, three. Ring the bell!" shouted the referee. The crowd went insane. They jumped, hollered, and nearly ripped the bleachers from the bolts in the wall.

They patted me on the back and beamed their approval as I limped my way back to the locker room. Halfway there, Bruno called into the mike, "Hey hotshot. You think you're pretty bad pinning a guy who's knocked out cold, don't you? I want a rematch. Two weeks from tonight. Right here. I wanna show these hillbilly rednecks what a real man can do."

All heads turned to me. "Two weeks from tonight?" I huffed. "What's wrong with right now?" I ran toward Bruno who dropped the mike causing earsplitting reverberation to echo through the hall. He ran toward me and we locked up like two longhorn bulls, brawling all the way through the dressing room doors. The fans about wet their pants in delight.

In the locker room we embraced, then shook hands. "Great match," Bruno said.

"Yeah, we really had 'em popping, didn't we," I said trying to catch my breath.

We dried off with towels lent to us by the gym teacher, peeling off wet, sticky layers of athletic tape, and tights, and kneepads. Outside, we could hear the crowd popping to the sounds of the next match.

I dressed slowly, feeling the ache in my joints and hearing my bones pop. You can't fake the falls either. Tony clambered through the room that was now heavy with the smell of fresh sweat and handed me my pay envelope—twenty bucks, enough to cover gas. I walked toward the exit door.

"Hey, Johnny," Bruno called after me. "Wanna get something to eat at IHOP?"

"Sure. I'll wait for you," I said sauntering toward the door. I stopped and turned devilishly. "Oh, and Bruno, remember the girl in the white dress?" I asked.

"Yeah," he said with a leering grin.

"She *didn't* have on any panties...and she wasn't a she!"

SUNLIGHT AND SHADOWS

I chase happiness
like a shadow
grasping at it
as it moves
inexorably
shrinking
in the noonday sun
until there's only
heat and
scraps of shade.

But soon the shadow
lengthens.
My heart lifts as
I reach again
and grab
and look in surprise as
my hands come up
empty.
I look up to question God
and find the sun
obscured
and under my feet
the grass is green and
darkened.

I look around
and notice
the world is so bright
beyond the shade.
I reach to seize
the sunlight
but clutch only air
and I stamp my foot
in frustration
at life's injustice.

—*Pamela Armstrong Stockwell*

22-MORT

YARD GAMES

John Bolin

It must have been solar flares that caused the madness to start. That's the only explanation I've ever been able to come up with. Great fire storms on the surface of the sun that somehow disrupted the laws of nature ninety-three million miles down here on Earth. I've read that such phenomenon screw up radio waves and mess with the weather. Maybe when a solar storm occurs, the whole earth gets knocked half a bubble out of plumb.

Whatever it was, something caused it because it definitely happened. And, when it was there, you knew it was there and when it was over, you knew it was gone. Whatever it was, it affected everybody and everything that happened in 1958.

Everything just went nuts that year —and stayed nuts till about 1960. Nothing worked in '58 and everything that ever had worked, broke. Everybody who had a good job either got laid off or fired. All the cotton mills in downtown Spartanburg had run twenty-four hours a day, seven days a week since the bombing of Pearl Harbor and every one of them shut down in 1958. As my stepfather phrased it, "Half the town is on starvation."

The summer of '58 was the hottest and driest summer I've ever known and the winter of that year was the coldest winter of my life. Every cow and every well went dry that summer; every water pipe that was buried less than two feet underground froze and busted that February. Lightening stuck the Methodist church on Reidville Road on the 4th of July and damn near burned it to the ground. I've wrestled with the theological implications of that ever since.

Two of the ugliest automobiles ever produced fell off the assembly lines that year like buckets of rotten squash: the Ford Easel and the Chevrolet Del Ray. With it's horse-collar grill, the Easel looked like an Oldsmobile sucking a lemon and the Del Ray looked like Detroit's reaction to phenolamide. Both were incredibly misconceived, mechanical road-toads. Of course, we had a 1958 six cylinder, straight drive, Chevrolet Del Ray—with blackwall tires. My brother hated it. "That damned car wouldn't pull a greasy string out of a rat's ass," were his exact words.

The entire social order seemed to unravel that year. Baptist preachers ran off with piano players, daughters of the pillars of our neighborhood society turned up pregnant. Bright boys—for no compelling reasons—quit school and joined the Marines. Good children ran away from home. Hail storms, floods, draughts, forest fires, slugs, tornadoes, infectious hepatitis, rubella. I kept listening for a voice: "Let my people go."

The Klan burned crosses in the cornfields behind my house. Lester Wolfe, one of my classmates, ran off with the circus—and literally got eaten by a lion. Somehow, all of a sudden, we were all bound and gagged in the back of a runaway beer truck heading the wrong direction off the on ramp on the highway of life. Madness was in the air.

In a single day in June of that year—more like a typical day matter of fact—my four year old half-sister managed to get into a bottle of my step father's "nerve pills", wolfed down a couple of dozen and went immediately off to *never-never* land.

My step father was on the back porch working on the washing machine when my mama screamed, "THE BABY'S DEAD." It's amazing how much commotion those three words can cause.

As my stepfather tried to get up to see what was going on, he managed to short out the 110-volt electric power supply to the washing machine with his wedding ring. When my mama got to the porch screaming for help with what she believed to be a dead child, she found my step father vibrating in the corner with his eyes rolled back in his head and a gold wedding ring sizzling on his finger. The voltage knocked both his shoes off.

My mama ran outside to get the car and found it sitting in the driveway with four flat tires. Tom Martin, my stepfather, had somehow managed to run over a ten penny nail laced two by four that *somebody* had left in the driveway the night before. She threw the baby in the front seat, jumped under the steering wheel and drove five miles to the hospital—flapping flat tires and all.

All this time, I was behind the barn digging fishing worms so I'd missed most of the action. John Ervin, my next door neighbor, came over after my mama blasted away in the Del Ray.

"Your mama is about as nuts as my old lady," he said.

"Whatcha mean?" I asked.

"Your mama just drove out of your driveway like Fireball Roberts. Your step-daddy ought to do something about the tires on that nasty Chevrolet. I know he's a tight son of a bitch but, Jesus H. Christ, the last time I looked, air was free."

Everybody survived that day but it was just one of many such days that year. Something like 700 days of sheer madness—and it lasted till about 1960.

The morning that my sister got out of the hospital, eight or ten of us "little ones" were playing in my back yard. There were two groups of kids in my neighborhood—"little ones" and "big boys." Thinking about it, we had the weirdest neighborhood. There were probably 25 boys in the West View community and I bet there wasn't five years difference in the ages of any of us. There was a big group of "little ones" and a smaller group of "big boys." There were only half dozen girls in the whole neighborhood, but that's another story altogether.

As I was saying, there were eight or ten of us in my back yard playing barefoot, suicide stretch, a variation of stretch. Stretch is a yard game. I'll explain: Two boys would stand face to face about five feet apart. Taking turns, each boy would attempt to throw a pocket, paring or butcher knife and stick it in the ground not more than six or eight inches from the outside of his opponent's foot. If you were successful in sticking the knife in the ground, your opponent was required to leave one foot stationary and move the other foot to the spot were the knife was sticking in the ground. A proficient player could, with just a few well-placed throws, "stretch" his opponent to the limit. Hence, the name "stretch". The game ended when one player could not stretch far enough to reach the knife or when he lost his balance.

My mama said she could tell whether or not the games we played originated on one of the mill hills around town. She said that if a game tended to break your arm or knock out your front teeth, it probably came off the hill. She said if a game resulted in at least one cast, a couple of broken teeth—and if a fistfight was an integral activity—it definitely came off the hill. If the game required cars and loaded guns, it came off the hill at Saxon Mill. Stretch came off the hill.

Over time, variations to the game of stretch evolved. One such variation was barefoot suicide stretch. In that particular variation, you started the game barefoot and in a full stretch/split position. Instead of stretching your opponent, the object of this particular variation was to avoid sticking your opponent in the foot as you moved his feet back toward one another with each throw—of an ice pick. An ice pick was the only acceptable piece of equipment in barefoot, suicide stretch.

We called it suicide stretch because the loser was the person that first misjudged the throw and nailed his opponent's foot to the ground. Moving your opponent's feet closer and closer together with each throw meant somebody would eventually get stuck. Happened every time. Once you entered into a game of barefoot, suicide stretch, you were absolutely, positively barred from getting out before either giving some blood or causing some bleeding. If you acted the least bit cavalier in losing, it usually cost you a fist in the mouth. Such were the rules in mill hill yard games. I've got freckles on the tops of both feet today from suicide stretch and I'm over 50 years old.

We were all watching John Ervin win another game of bare-foot, suicide stretch with cross-eyed Peter Johnson when Gregg Mann, a friend of my brother showed up. Peter was real cross-eyed. My mama said he was so cross-eyed that he could lay flat on his back and still look down the well. John Ervin was the only kid in the neighborhood who would play stretch with Peter, much less play suicide stretch with him. Peter always lost, sometimes on the first throw. You'd see a kid with an ice pick sticking out of his thigh and you'd know that Peter had lost another game.

Peter had just managed to stick an ice pick between John Ervin's toes—narrowly avoiding another loss—when Gregg Mann strolled across the yard and distracted our attention. He had a hunting bow in his hand. It drew us like iron filings to a magnet.

"Look what my brother brought me back from Atlanta." Gregg held up a hunting bow.

"God damn, it's a hunting bow," exclaimed John Ervin. "I saw one just like that in *Field and Stream*. I bet that thing will shoot half a fucking mile. Let me shoot it."

The hunting bow caused quite a commotion. None of us had ever seen a real hunting bow before. We'd made bows and we'd made arrows. Lots of times. But they never performed like they were supposed to. It never was a mystery to me why the Indians lost out to the cowboys. You couldn't hit the broad side of a barn with a homemade bow and arrow. The only thing I ever hit solid was my stepfather's 1954 Ford. I was aiming at the barn.

We spent the rest of the afternoon shooting Gregg's bow. We made targets and put them on bales of hay and shot till the hay bales would no longer stop the arrows. We shot long shots, short shots, moving targets. We shot that 30 pound bow till we had blisters on our fingers. About 7:30 that evening, just as the sun was going down, we were all standing around in the back yard when Gregg said, "Watch this."

And with that, he pulled an arrow back till the tip touched

the bow, pointed the arrow straight up and let it fly. We all watched the arrow zip into the twilight until it disappeared. It dawned on all of us at the same time, "What goes up . . ." General panic!

Everybody started running at the same time. Kids dove under the car, under the edge of the barn, John Ervin grabbed a number-three tin tub and held it over his head. I dove in the doorway of our well house. The arrow came to earth about twenty feet from Gregg and stuck in the yard. Great fun. The gang would gather, Gregg would catch everybody off guard and he'd yell, "Arrow up!" and fire away. We'd scatter like chickens. Everybody except Gregg.

Gregg never ran like the rest of us. He'd shoot and stand still. Gregg said he didn't have to get out of the way. "All you chicken shit little wuzzies can run and hide but I ain't."

In some sort of mill hill, cotton mill-loom-fixer logic, Gregg theorized that since a launched arrow had the entire earth to fall back to, the chances were slim to none that it would fall exactly back to it's launch site. Lightening not striking the same place twice and arrows not going exactly straight up or falling exactly straight back to the same spot made plenty of sense to Gregg. He was safe. No doubt in his mind.

It was almost dark when Gregg let loose the last arrow of the evening. "Arrow up," he yelled. Kids ran in all directions. Gregg stood perfectly still. The arrow zipped about 300 yards straight up and out of sight. It fell back to earth just as fast as a thirty-six inch steel tipped arrow can fall and hit Gregg Mann—and stuck in his head.

I'll never forget it. I'd hopped under the edge of the well house and I wasn't ten feet from Gregg. I saw it hit him. It hit him—and it stuck in his head. When all the kids came out of hiding to see Gregg, it must have looked like the midget scene from Wizard of Oz after the house fell on the witch with the ruby shoes.

At first, I don't think Gregg realized what had happened. His eyes rolled up toward his forehead and he reached up with both hands to try to determine what had just hit him. When his hands touched the arrow shaft, he froze. A trickle of blood ran down between his eyes and started to drip off the tip of his nose. Gregg touched his nose and looked at the blood on his fingers. He turned to Jell-O and he fell to his knees.

"I'm shot. I'm shot. Oh God, I'm shot." Gregg was screaming. Kids flew like quail!

I decided it was time to get my mama involved. She was pretty good at this sort of stuff. God knows, she had enough practice. I dashed for the back door and ran headlong into my mama coming out of the kitchen.

I screamed, "Gregg Mann's killed hisself with a arrow. It's sticking out of his head and his brains are running out of his nose. Me and John Ervin didn't have nothing to do with it. We told him not to shoot hisself."

That probably wasn't the best way to break the news to my mama but it did get her undivided attention. Mama leaped out the back door and hit the ground running. Kids were crying, dogs were barking, Gregg was screaming. It was something to see.

"Jesus, merciful God," my mama said, "what have you done to yourself?"

"I've got an arrow stuck in my head and I'm dying," Gregg screamed.

Now Gregg Man did in fact have an arrow stuck in his head. The falling arrow with the steel tip didn't have enough force to actually crack Gregg's skull but it did have sufficient force to break the skin when it hit him and slip between his skull and scalp, traveled five or six inches and finally stopped below his ear. As scalp wounds will, this one produced a good bit of blood so it looked a lot worse than it actually was. He was in some pain and he was scared to death.

My mama could see from the angle of the arrow and from the ridge behind Gregg's ear that the arrow had not penetrated his skull and I think she knew that his life was probably not in danger. She was probably more concerned about his emotional than his physical state. Mama attempted to pull the arrow out of Gregg's head but when she touched the shaft, he protested so that she reconsidered. "Put him in Lus's truck and we'll take him to the hospital," she said. Lus Miller was our next door neighbor.

The closest emergency room was on the other side of town at the Spartanburg Memorial Hospital, about five or six miles away. My stepfather had already left for work so Mama got the keys from Lus's wife while we dealt with Gregg. We couldn't get him in the cab because the arrow hit the roof. We started to break the arrow in half but Gregg pitched a fit so we put him in the truck bed.

To get to the hospital, we had to drive completely through town. I'll never forget the ride down Pine Street Extension to the emergency room. Mama was driving like a bat out of hell and there were six or eight of us kids either in the cab or in the back with Gregg. Gregg was sitting in the back of the truck with an arrow sticking right out of the top of his head. Blood was running between his eyes and dripping off the end of his nose. By the time we got halfway to the hospital, all the kids in the truck bed were splattered. When my mama was forced to slow down, cars would pull up behind us—and you could see the drivers' expressions flash when they realized what they were seeing. Couple of them just drove off in the ditch. One old man damned near ran Mama off the road trying to get her to pull over. He ran up beside her and yelled that there was a boy in the back of the truck with a stick stuck in his head. Mama just drove.

The emergency room scene wasn't much better. When Mama drove into the emergency room parking lot, she told my brother to run inside and get some help. My brother took her at her word and before the truck stopped he bailed out and ran for the front desk yelling that there was a dead boy in the back of a pickup truck in the parking lot. That got everybody's attention.

All the kids who rode in the truck sat out on the curb in front of the hospital and waited for the doctor to extract the arrow from Gregg Mann's head. Mama said she would kill the first kid who moved. The tone of her voice kept me sitting on the curb for the duration.

I had never seen a street light come on before that night on the corner of California Avenue across the street from a drive-in called Jimmy's in Spartanburg in the mad summer of 1958. That year was only the beginning.

REMEMBERING GEORGE

I stood among those who loved you.
Saw the top of your head, like a brown nest,
Peeking out amid the roses and carnations
That draped your open casket.
Your head will never see a gray hair.
Your body, strong and steady as a sailing ship
Betrayed you mid-voyage.

Will you hear me?
If I tell you how your smile filled the room
How your laugh spread like seeds
In a breath of April wind?

And when you looked at the one who shared your life,
Your eyes shone like stars too brilliant for night,
And I was a student of those eyes
They taught me how important

It is to love.

—*Carla Damron*

2-MORT

BETWEEN THE SLATS

Frances Jones

The teacher and I herded our little four-year old lambs in an almost straight line, like sheep in a fresh green pasture. They sat on the front row of the sanctuary, whispering excitedly about promotion day.

We shushed and whispered, motioning our silent commands, waving our hands and flapping our arms up and down in silent awkward motions, reminding our little lambs of the "do's" and "don'ts" of perfect behavior on promotion day. In spite of their soft giggles, they listened.

"Don't laugh out loud."

"Don't pick your nose."

"Don't talk."

"Don't kick the seat in front of you."

"Don't dangle your feet."

"Don't kick your seatmate."

"Don't pull his hair."

"Don't jerk Mary's curls."

"Don't stand up in your seat to wave to your parents behind you."

"Please, please don't sigh out loud if the minister prays too long."

The choir's loud singing drowned out most of the giggling. Not too bad for four-year olds.

The minister stood and prayed. He prayed and prayed. Then he prayed some more. And some more.

At one point I gently reached for my son's little hand and squeezed it to let him know how proud he made me feel and how pleased I was that he was quiet, unlike some of the other children. He squeezed my hand back before I let go of his.

The minister continued to pray. And pray.

"Amen," the minister said at last. He then launched into his sermon.

I opened my eyes, startled to see my son's head wedged between the slats of a straight chair that stood near the front pew. I gasped and quickly made my way over to where my son struggled to free himself.

I took his head in my hands and carefully twisted it to the side in an attempt to force it through the slats. His head didn't budge. I turned it to the opposite side. His head still didn't budge. I lifted the chair, stretching my son's neck in the process. His head remained trapped in the chair.

My son began to cry softly as people began to whisper and murmur. Some even began to laugh.

"What's wrong," our assistant minister whispered rhetorically as he came down from the chancel and slipped toward my son. Reaching him, the assistant minister did as I had done, including lifting the chair and stretching my son's neck. All for naught. As before, my son's head stayed caught between the slats.

The assistant minister's failed efforts caused my son's soft cries to become loud shrieks. The loud shrieks halted the minister's sermon.

The minister stepped away from the pulpit and walked to where the assistant minister still held the chair that held my son's head. Taking charge, the minister pointed to his assistant, "You pick up the boy. I'll pick up the chair."

After a few twists and turns, my son's head, as if by some miracle popped free and he immediately stopped screaming.

Everybody applauded and sat back in their pews. The minister returned to the pulpit to complete his sermon.

When he finished, he bowed his head and began praying again. I bowed my head also, but this time I did not close my eyes.

DEFINITIONS
OR
GREAT (UNREALISTIC)
EXPECTATIONS

Trust:
Confidence in the honesty, integrity and reliability of another,
With the attendant anticipation, expectation and hope for the future.
The responsibility and obligation resulting from the confidence placed in one.
Credit, and the confidence in one's future ability to pay.
Something placed with one for safekeeping,
Or a cartel or monopoly.
Property administered for the benefit of another.
To have faith, place reliance and be confident,
And to believe in another's honesty, integrity and justice.
To Allow one to do something without fear of the outcome.
Expecting confidently.
To rely.

Betrayal:
To expose to the enemy, traitorously.
To break the faith with.
To fail to meet the hopes of.
To lead astray.
To deceive.

To seduce and then desert.
To reveal against another's wishes.
To indicate.
To disclose, even unwillingly.
To deceive and reveal.
To help the enemy.

There he is and he did it.
I can't stand you anymore.
You've changed.
They made me do it.
I was playing golf.
I'll love you forever and ever.
I can see it in your face.
He's the one.
All right, I did it.
Of course I won't tell anybody.
She went that way.
I am so lonely.

—*Ann Furr*

CLEANING HOUSE

Pamela Armstrong Stockwell

Cathy stared at the miniature footprints that marched across the pale carpet. Each little whorl of tread threw tinder on the fire of anger welling up inside her. Dammit! she thought. Why can't he just take off his shoes like she's told him a million times?

She glanced around the rest of the room. Everything else was as it should be. Mail stacked neatly on the table, glass tables clear of dust, sofa cushions just so. Thank God. She had been through housekeeper after housekeeper, trying to find one with standards close to hers, and Ellen was the best she could find. But she had gone for the day and so had missed this little mess. It would be up to Cathy to clean it up.

Cathy's house was her life. It represented an enormous investment of time and effort, and it had been the means by which she removed herself from her past. She had sold her youth for this house. She had gotten her G.E.D. at sixteen and her master's degree by twenty-two. After college, she worked twelve hours a day—and sometimes more—six and seven days a week, offering up her youth as the supreme sacrifice to appease the gods of righteousness and homeowning. Now at thirty-four, she had her own firm and this house. Her home was her sanctuary. Clean and bright and spacious. But no one respected her desire to keep it that way. She struggled with her husband and her son, trying desperately—and apparently fruitlessly—to get them to keep the place neat and clean.

"Josh!" she yelled.

2-MORT

Running footsteps echoed down the hall and a small boy ran into the room. "Hi, Mommy!" he said, as he prepared to launch his four-year-old body at her. Her frozen look slowed him down. He saw her look at the carpet and his gaze followed hers. He saw the footprints.

"I'm sorry, Mommy," he said, his eyes beginning to sparkle as tears pooled and threatened to flood. "I tried to tiptoe." Cathy did notice that the footprints were only half prints. But they still marred her carpet.

"That's not good enough, Josh," she said. "I told you not to come in here with muddy feet. Didn't I? Didn't I tell you that?"

"Yes, ma'am."

"Why do you continue to do this? I don't know what to do. I tell you over and over, and you just don't listen. I'm at my wits' end." She sucked in her breath, feeling the anger pulsing like a dark, malignant heart.

"Just go on up to your room. I'll talk to you more about this later."

He turned to go upstairs, his small shoulders slumped. She noticed he was in his stocking feet. Now he takes them off, she thought, and the anger flared.

When Paul came home from work, she stood at the stove cooking dinner. As soon as he walked in, her simmering anger bubbled over and flooded the kitchen.

"I've had Josh in his room all day," she said, stirring a beef stew with quick, sharp strokes of a wooden spoon. "He left tracks on my carpet again. I am sick and tired of you and him not caring a thing about this house. I work, too, you know. And I come home early from a meeting and find my house a mess. I'm sick and tired of it." She slammed the lid on the pot and the stove rattled as if it, too, trembled in the face of her wrath.

Paul stood for a moment, briefcase in hand. She heard him sigh. "I'm fine, honey. Thanks for asking. And how are you?"

She shot him a withering look. He hated confrontation and

tried to keep a bit of humor hovering somewhere on the fringes of their arguments. Sometimes it helped. Tonight it didn't.

Cathy served the stew over rice, complemented by a salad and generous helpings of tension. The subdued Josh sat at the table stabbing bits of potato with his fork. Usually bubbly and irrepressible, this intelligent, good-natured child was sensitive to his mother's moods. He returned to normal only when she did.

The silent meal wound to an uncomfortable close. As usual, Paul helped Cathy clear the table and do the dishes while Josh went to the family room to watch TV. Cathy avoided meeting Paul's eyes. Hostility still radiated off her like heat from a bonfire.

"I'm meeting Becky for lunch tomorrow," she said, using a fork to scrape food off a plate and into the garbage disposal. She jabbed it with the tines to make sure it all went down.

"Oh, good. It's been, what? Fifteen years since you've seen her?"

She felt the edges of her anger soften just a little. "Eighteen. She lives just a few miles from here. I'm having lunch at her house. She said it would be easier because of Donny."

"Oh, God, I always forget. He's got some kind of muscle disease, doesn't he?"

"Yes. I looked it up one time. Duchenne muscular dystrophy. It's fatal. Donny'll just keep getting weaker and weaker, until . . ." she shook her head. She began washing the large stewpot, scrubbing the sides with a vengeance. "Anyway, I'm looking forward to seeing her. I'll take Josh with me."

Paul touched her shoulder gently. "Cathy," he said softly. "I love you. I wish you wouldn't let little things get under your skin."

She suppressed a flair of irritation. Why couldn't he understand that, to her, the "little things" weren't little things. Really, it was like talking to a wall sometimes.

The next day, she found herself appreciating the scenery as she drove down the winding mountain road to Becky's new house on the other side of the river. An early morning downpour had yielded

2-MORT

to a bright, blue sky. The rain had left sun-struck droplets on the autumn leaves that magnified the brilliant hues. She glanced at the neighboring ridges, marveling at the beauty. *So like our home way back when.*

Her mind drifted back to the little ridge that had been her world for sixteen years. One could look out at breathtaking views, but up close, all one saw was hardscrabble yards and soil so full of rocks that only the toughest plants put down roots. Her father had worked with Becky's in the coal mines. Both girls had grown up in houses permeated with coal dust. The grime from the mines had settled into her father's pores so that it was like a second skin. Her mother had bad nerves, they said. Cathy often wondered what a real doctor—not that sorry, drunken excuse for a general practitioner that they depended on—would say about her mother's condition. Depression? Chronic fatigue syndrome?

Whatever it had been, the house had languished in filth. Torn, battered, second-hand furniture and piles of unwashed, coal-dust-streaked laundry filled the small rooms; dirt lacquered the floors; the tacky residue of countless meals covered the kitchen counters like contact paper. Although dirt darkened the windows, her mother often closed the curtains on her "bad days," adding gloom to the grime. But beyond the blackened glass lay rolling mountains that taunted Cathy with their pure beauty.

Becky's house had been a little cleaner, but Cathy had decided that no house in a coal mining town could ever be clean. The fine, black, greedy dust left nothing untouched. She remembered one Easter Sunday when she had gotten a new, lacy white dress that made her feel like a princess. By the time church was over, the dress had a grayish cast and smudges from her fingers marked the skirt. When she got home, she tore off the dress and burned it. Her mother never asked about the dress, and Cathy never asked for a new one. She left home as soon as she could and never looked back. *Until now*, she thought ruefully.

Still, she looked forward to seeing Becky again after all these years. They had exchanged Christmas cards and occasional phone calls but hadn't seen each other since Cathy left home. Cathy couldn't believe so much time had gone by.

She soon spotted Becky's red brick house, recognizing it from her friend's description. She felt her heart contract when she saw the wheelchair ramp leading to the front door. *God, that's awful,* she thought. Poor Becky.

When Becky opened the door, Cathy had no trouble recognizing the girl who peeked out from the face of the woman before her. Becky still wore her blonde hair long, her eyes still danced, and she was still one of the smallest people Cathy had ever met. Cathy had to search for the lines around the eyes that bore witness to the eighteen-year gulf that lay between the shores of their girlhood and the place they now found themselves.

Becky squealed. "My God, Cathy! You look great!" She hugged her and stood her at arm's length and then hugged her again.

Cathy laughed. "So do you! I thought you would have grown up by now."

"I always was the runt." She opened the door wider. "Come in. This must be Josh." She bent down to get a better look at him. He sidled closer to his mom, but grinned.

"You're my mom's friend," he said, knowingly.

Becky laughed. "I sure am."

Cathy heard a soft whir of an electric motor. A thin boy zoomed into the room in an electric wheelchair. Her heart flip-flopped again. Josh was almost as big as he was, even though Cathy knew that Donny was 10 years old. Donny kept one frail hand on the wheelchair's joy stick, and the other lay in his lap as if carelessly tossed there. Straps held his small frame upright. But his face projected mischief and life.

"Donny, this is Miss Cathy."

"Hi," he said, and she saw the bright curiosity in his eyes.

"Nice to meet you, Donny," Cathy said

"Is this your little boy?" he asked.

"Yes, this is Josh." Josh's eyes widened at the sight of the boy and his contraption. With a small adept movement of his hand, Donny rolled directly in front of Josh. "Hi, Josh. Wanna play?"

"I want to ride that," Josh said, pointing at the chair. Cathy flushed, but before she could reply, Becky said, "I'm afraid Donny needs that chair to get around. He can't walk like you or me. His muscles are sick."

"Oh. I hope they get better soon. Then I can ride, right?"

"We'll see," Becky said. "Why don't you take him outside to play, Donny? Stay in the front yard."

As they went out the door and down the ramp, Cathy turned to Becky. "You sure they'll be OK?"

Becky closed the screen door but left the wooden door open. "Positive. Donny knows the rules about staying in the yard. Don't worry."

They sat on the sofa and sipped iced tea as they caught up. Becky talked about her husband's job that had taken them to Cincinnati and back after several years and about trying to find a school that could accommodate Donny's needs. Cathy talked about her public relations firm, her husband's career as a manager of a textile company and how he supported her and Josh.

They paused every now and again to check on the two boys, who played together, happily oblivious to the adults' concern.

At one o'clock, Becky called them in for lunch. Donny's chair stuck in some mud long enough for Josh to get a good head start. He tore up the ramp, his gamin face flushed, his hair damp with the sweet sweat of childhood. As Josh dashed in the house, he left behind him a trail of muddy sneaker prints.

"Josh! What have I told you about wiping your feet? They're filthy," Cathy said, teeth clenched as she tried to keep her voice down. Josh skidded to a halt, leaving a long streak of reddish-brown clay on the hardwood floor.

Becky smiled. "Don't worry, Cathy. It's going to get a whole lot worse in a minute. Josh, I put some phone books in a chair for you."

Donny zoomed into the room and instantly slowed the chair.

He wheeled slowly into the dining room and joined Josh.

In his wake, he left four overlapping ribbons of mud.

Cathy felt like a hand held her throat. She fought down the urge to look for a broom and mop. *It's not my house*, she told herself. *I don't have to worry about it.*

Josh dug into his food enthusiastically. Becky settled herself near Donny and began feeding him. Cathy tried not to stare, but the whole process fascinated and surprised her. Donny accepted his food without embarrassment. Josh ate, oblivious to anything.

After dinner, the boys went back outside, and Cathy helped Becky clear the table. "Can I help you clean this?" Cathy asked, looking at the floor.

Becky shrugged. "Not until they finish playing."

"This would drive me crazy," Cathy said, with a nervous laugh. "How do you put up with it?"

Becky looked out the window at the two boys. Each had a stick that served as a make-believe gun. They chased each other around the yard, shrieking and whooping.

"It used to bother me," she said. "We tried putting a carpet in front of the door and having him run the wheelchair back and forth over it. But it didn't really work. Now, I just don't think it's worth it. I won't have much time with Donny. I don't want to spend it all yelling at him."

Cathy silently watched the boys. Donny's stick fell out of his lap, and Josh immediately ran to pick it up. He placed it under Donny's left hand gently and said something to him. Donny nodded, reversed his chair and the two took off. She sensed she had seen something important, like some great truth was pushing against her subconscious, but she couldn't quite grasp it.

After they returned home later that afternoon, Cathy sat on the sofa, rifling through the mail. Josh ran into the room, dipping and waving his chubby, outstretched arms.

"Josh, stop running around like that! You're going to break

something," she said, without emphasis. He apparently noticed her lack of conviction because he didn't break stride or stop the humming that she supposed represented his imitation of an airplane in flight.

Just as she tore open an envelope, a crash made her jerk her head up.

The crash put the brakes on Josh's flight. He stood in a patch of sunlight that poured in through the window. His put his index finger on his trembling bottom lip and his eyes filled with tears.

Suddenly Cathy pictured how Becky might have reacted. Would she have yelled at Donny? Or punished him? Cathy didn't think so. She remembered Josh placing the twig so gently under Donny's useless hand. Then she knew what it was she couldn't quite see earlier. She had not worked so hard for this house. The house was a shell. She had worked for her husband, and this sweet, kind generous child. What was more important than making sure he grew up and kept those virtues?

She reached down to her son and gathered him in her arms, hugging him tight. Then she held him at arms length and kissed his cheeks "Are you all right? Did you get hurt?"

"N-no," he stammered. "I'm OK. You're not mad at me?"

"No, honey, I'm not mad. I'm not mad at all."

PROSE POEM IN MONOSYLLABLES

(This was written to be read aloud.)

Shrimp leap in the ebb tide of the salt marsh. An old black man throws a cast net. It spins wide and taut, lands with a splash, and is drawn closed. A tall girl in a blue dress looks down from the bridge, as the old man pulls the wet mesh with the trapped shrimp from the brine. A gull lands on the bridge rail, and the girl smiles as it cocks its head to the side and looks to her like a new found friend.

The girl squints from the bright sun in the clear sky and says, "Hi, bird! I wish I could fly. I'd take to the air and fly up high where the land looks like a big quilt." The gull blinks, but it looks like a wink to the tall girl on the bridge. Then it hops from the rail and rides the wind to a mud flat in the salt marsh, to look for a meal.

The girl looks at the old man as he dumps his catch in a big pail. He has all the shrimp he needs for a meal. Up since dawn, he's hot and tired, and yearns for a cold beer. He sees the girl on the bridge and waves. The girl waves back and thinks of the shrimp in the man's pail. Packed in the pail they can't leap and they can't swim, and it's not fair; but a man has to eat as sure as a gull. That's life, she thinks as she turns from the rail and heads up the road from the low bridge to have lunch on the beach with her dad.

The old man folds the net and drapes it on the pail. He hefts his catch and slogs through the mud, then walks up the bank from the creek to the road, which is hot from the noon sun. He thinks of his house down a dirt road, and his fat wife who's a good cook and his best friend. He'll wash up and start on a beer while she boils the shrimp. Then they'll sit down and peel the while the grits and greens cook on the stove.

It's a hot day and he runs sweat and his joints ache as he totes the pail down the road towards home. We don't have much, he thinks as he walks, but the shrimps are free for a man with a net, and the roof don't leak, and my wife's a good old girl. With shrimp and grits, fresh greens, hot sauce, a cold beer, and a long nap…it's a good life.

—*Jeff Koob*

MORNING GLORY

Ann Furr

The morning glory grew up the trellis outside the window in the same season it had for all the years that it had been there, yet, this year it was different. The leaves grew the same size and shape, but the color had changed. The leaves, green for as long as anyone's memory stretched, were now deep purple with broad bands of iridescent gold outlining the edges. The blossoms came in their season, but instead of the uniform lilac, each bloom unfolded with a different brilliant hue, a pure color, with glimmering gold marking the edges.

I stood and stared at the strange vine with its bell-shaped flowers. The appearance of the plant sent rays of excitement down my spine and made chill bumps pop out all over me with such force that I had to stop looking. Papa said the strange colors came because John had poured the cooking grease too close to the vine, but Mama saw the miraculous plant as a sign that portended change. I knew Mama was right.

That spring things began to happen. Molly stuck a thorn in her great toe and nothing would pull the infection out. The toe swelled up as big as a lemon and as red as a ripe tomato and, like the ripe tomato, it looked as though it would split right open if it were bumped. She hobbled around and, when she did bump the toe thick white pus shot in a great arc out of the place where the thorn went in, landing in a gluey mass against a wall. Mama cried that her baby would die. But Papa said that nature takes care of thorns and babies.

One day Molly, who was only four, picked one of the purple and gold leaves (the rest of the family had been afraid to even touch the bizarre plant) and before anyone knew took a large bite from the leaf. With the whole family screaming in fright, she sat down in the rain and crumpled the rest of the leaf, squeezing the juice onto her toe and into the suppurated hole where the thorn had penetrated. By evening her toe resumed its normal size and color and Molly could even bend it and walk normally again.

After that, everything began to change. At once thrilling and frightening, the change swirled up around us and twisted and twirled us faster and faster.

Mama began serving foods of only one color on any day. Meals weren't so bad when she chose a common color like green. We ate turnip greens and cabbage chopped into a slaw or kraut, a few bread and butter pickles on the side, a big lettuce salad, and lime jello for dessert. Sometimes she chose red and we would have beets beside the red raw meat, catsup and sliced tomatoes and sometimes strawberries for dessert. If the sky was overcast, we had brown food, speckled butter beans, black-eyed peas, lentils, meat loaf, brown rice, and dark brown bread. On the holy days and Sundays, Mama would insist that we eat only white things. We would have white bread, with the brown crust carefully cut off, turkey or white chicken meat, grits or mashed potatoes (with only milk gravy), and maybe some white beans or hominy. On those days, we waited for the fresh coconut cake to appear for dessert.

As the summer wore on, mother got more and more creative with her dinners. On a midweek orange day, we had piles of day lily blooms neatly sautéed and sliced, next to the mashed sweet potatoes and across from the diced carrots. With each new burst of color Mama became more and more convinced that this was the only proper and healthy way to eat and soon our drinks appeared color coded, too. On Sundays and Holy Days we drank only milk; on green days, lime Kool Aid.

Then Mama insisted that she needed plates to match the food. Assembling the dishes for each color took a while. Looking on the green meals served on green plates with the tall green glasses of lime green Kool Aid all resting on a lovely green table cloth, with a bouquet of greenery in a green vase in the center of the table comforted Mama.

The whole family began to act like the color of the foods we ate. On yellow days, our family would be sunny and cheerful, but on red days, fire shot amongst us the whole day. A white day usually followed, and each family member folded peacefully into himself and calmness prevailed.

On the fifteenth of July, the afternoon came up hot and humid and the dense air weighed down heavily upon us. The atmosphere seemed to hold you to the earth, pressing on your shoulders. Suddenly, the barometric pressure changed and the hot air got light.

My sister, Becky, was out in the chicken yard with corn in her apron when the wind picked up and swirled Becky's long, red hair, which hung below her waist. Then the air stilled and a noise began. At first the noise purred like a cat, but then it built up to a roar, like a mountain lion, and before I knew what was happening the noise sounded like a train.

I looked up and saw the gray funnel in the sky swirl towards us. Then I understood. I screamed to Becky to run over to the barn, but it was no use because she couldn't hear me above the howling. I saw the funnel cloud get right over her, dip down with its tip, and suck pick her up with the corn and her red hair whirling around her. The spinning, yowling wind swept her low through the trees and out of sight.

I ran after her, hysterical, following her path marked by the long, red strands of hair entangled in the trees. I saw her ahead of me, dangling from a branch by the remaining strands of her red locks. Her feet almost touched the ground, yet, she made no effort to get down, content to sway gently in the wind, limp, her hands at her sides.

She stared after the wind, as if saddened by its departure without her. I climbed the tree and pushed the branch down until her feet touched the ground, and she crumpled into a heap. I picked her up, carrying and dragging her home, while she stared all the while after the wind.

Her hair had been pulled from the crown and the middle part leaving her bald. Only a few strands of her auburn hair remained and Mama fixed what was left to cover the bald spot. Becky never spoke another word. I guess that from that day the wind swooped her up it just blew right through her and whirled her soul and everything that she knew right out of her. From then on, she would sit for hours on her window seat and look out at the sky and make noises like the wind, whirling whooshing noises. She would stare at the sky begging the wind to come back and take her on another wonderful ride. Mama said she had been seduced by the wind.

Later in the summer, a big storm came with angry gray clouds, lightning and thunder, and high winds. Becky ecstatically watched it from her window, while making her low mournful wind sounds. As Mama walked from the barn, she saw Becky stand up in the window, plunge out into the wind, and come crashing to the ground, head first, all the time laughing and making wind noises. She died with her eyes wide open, staring into the wind as it carried away her soul.

Mama said that because Becky had fallen under the spell of flying with the wind she should be buried up in the air, in the wind, on a platform like the Indians used to do. But Papa wouldn't hear of it. So Becky was laid to rest in the family plot next to Grandmother.

Before we buried her, Mama cut off the rest of Becky's auburn hair and braided it into a necklace and if you hold that necklace up to your ear you can still hear the wind blow.

Mama could not be consoled and wept loudly. Papa was just as sad, but he never said a word, just carried that long melancholy face around all over the countryside. After that when the wind would blow it was just like Becky was right there again with us, just outside the house. Mama said she had gone to live with the wind and Mama would talk to Becky when the wind howled.

The first frost came and withered the morning glory vine. On that cold day, the beautiful hues suddenly turned black and the gold edges of the leaves were no more. The death of the vine seemed to portend the end of change.

At least for now.

22-MORT

GARNETT

You were amazing
with your violet eyes
that almost made observers
believe in aliens…
they turned to soft
doe brown and shine
today from a man's body,
tall and drop-dead handsome.
Only your mother remembers
those early morning hours when all
the blue-eyed nurses were in awe.

—*Righton H. McCallum*

BLACKHEART

Ann Furr

I see her in eerie meetings everywhere I go. The elevator door opens and I hobble in, head down. She is standing there, seemingly as shocked to see me, as I am to see her. I look at her—tall, lithe, shapely, with long auburn hair and the most fashionable clothes— and as I stare her entire body becomes transparent, like a gathering of lead crystal. Her curves remain smooth and gentle but with the hard solidity of glass, impenetrable yet easily shattered.

I want to look away, but I am mesmerized, trapped again. I am shocked to realize that her interior is transparent and so completely empty. Her core is sparkling in its clarity and contains not so much as a bubble except in the upper left side of her torso. There is the pulsating black lump that causes me to avert my eyes. It is the traditional valentine shape, but its shiny blackness is horrifying.

She knows what I can see and we are both embarrassed. What I see is shocking, but the fact that my eyes suddenly work in this new way is terrifying. When did my eyes change and why am I repeatedly subjected to this spectacle? I do not ask to see her as I do, beyond nakedness. I can only shudder at her reaction to this ultimate intrusion. Does she know that this whole episode is automatic, against my will? Surely she does not think it is deliberate, or does she? Where is she from and why is she here? Worse yet, why are we doomed to this silent intercourse?

2-MORT

I lift my eyes again to the black heart. Its rhythmic contractions increase slightly. In my terror I am uncertain. Is this her terror, or an anxious prelude to an attack? My hand tightens on my cane, my only defense. How much does she know about me? Can she see through me, read my mind? Does she know that I sometimes encounter other people who have been around her and that I can feel her black energy coming from them? The force emitted from her pulsating black valentine sticks to them and marks them, muddying their aura. This memory causes me to pull away from her. I cannot let her touch me.

She sees me take a backward step in the elevator and the black heart doubles its pace. Paralyzed with fear, I find myself trapped in the tiny compartment as she raises her arms and steps towards me. I close my eyes so tightly that I feel my face distort. I steady myself with my left arm against the back of the elevator and swing my cane with all my force towards her crystal head. I feel the impact and I feel and hear the glass shatter. I open my eyes slightly and I am rewarded with a rainbow of light as the crystal shards fall to the earth. To my horror I glimpse the black heart exposed and free, still pulsating on the floor. I turn and flee.

The next morning the newspaper carried two stories on the front page.

MOTHER OF THREE MURDERED

The community was shocked with the murder of Beth Mason, a young mother of three, late yesterday in the downtown parking garage. Her body was found in the elevator and the medical examiner has ruled that the cause of death was a blow to the head. Police are seeking anyone who may have been in the garage and seen anything. They have no motive and few clues....

ICE SCULPTURE DESTROYED

The chairman of the winter festival, voiced shock and dismay as she viewed the ruins of the ice sculpture on the courthouse lawn. A life-sized tableau entitled "The Black Heart" was shattered....

SOMEWHERE OUT OF SUEZ

When the minister intoned,
"She is not here…"
Indeed she was not
in any sense but
love and memories.
The corpus delecti
was in absentia
courtesy of the Postal Service
who misplaced her somewhere
between the crematorium
and the churchyard.
Most of those who grieved
never knew, but at least
one blamed it on *her*
for willing cremation
in the first place.
In some familiar ivory,
plastic box she journeys on
through unknown places.
The ironic consolation is…
she always loved to travel.

—*Righton H. McCallum*

TOY COUNTER ENCOUNTER[2]

Bert Goolsby

We left the picture show that Saturday after watching a cowboy hero and his funny sidekick each fire his six-shooter at bad guys more than eighty times without reloading, a gang of wisecracking New York City teenagers avoid yet another day of school and bring criminals to justice, cartoon characters gaily assault each other with explosives, shotgun blasts, and blows to the head, and a drugged, securely bound masked man encased in concrete inside an exploding munitions ship surely die (with his mask on and his identity thus preserved) before he could wake up, free himself, and swim to safety twenty-five miles away. As I paused for my eyes to adjust to the daylight, I glimpsed my short, box-shaped, tow-headed little brother dart across the street and run straight for the dime store.

He dodged past two farmers clad in bib overalls and hunkered down on the sidewalk, munching boiled peanuts from small, damp brown sacks. Empty hulls encircled their brogans. They appeared not to notice my brother, although he nearly knocked one of them over. Both men seemed dazzled by a street preacher who screamed passages from *The Revelation* to all sinners within earshot.

"And upon her forehead was a name written, MYSTERY," I heard him yell as my brother caught the revolving door and pushed his way inside. I overtook him moments later, having raced by the two farmers and the preacher. I found my brother exactly where I knew he would be—at the toy counter.

-MORT

A toy counter to my brother was like a church altar. When standing before one of these holy tables, he never failed to practice the ancient ritual of the laying-on-of-hands. He attempted to bless every toy within reach.

To this day, I've not seen another store clerk like her. If God indeed makes us what we are, God certainly did a good job with her. She was perfect for the toy counter. She stood at least six feet tall and must have weighed more than two hundred pounds. The black clothes she always wore made me hesitate more than once to look at the toys on display. I never saw her smile and I never heard her thank a kid for buying a toy. She'd make kids stand there a long time before she would wait on them. And if they didn't have the right change, she'd complain about it. She didn't like a lot of pennies either.

But what really made her perfect for the toy counter were the dark glasses she always wore. I never quite knew where she was looking or whom she was watching. Sometimes when I thought she was looking straight ahead, she'd really be looking to her left.

Many a time a kid would come up to the counter and, after glancing at where she was posted and being satisfied she was looking the other way, would pick up a toy and start playing with it only to be hollered at and told to put that toy down unless "you're gonna to buy it." She had a way of catching a kid off guard.

My brother, conscious of the baleful form on the other side but never appreciating the problem posed by the dark glasses, ran up to the toy counter to see what new delights it contained. His blue eyes barely cleared the top of the counter. He quickly spotted a yellow and blue toy he had not seen the weekend before. He peered up at the grave guardian looming nearby and concluded she was looking elsewhere. "Look," he whispered to me, "a motor-cycle policeman."

He peeked at the somber shape one more time and, believing everything was still safe, slowly reached and picked up the motor-cycle with the blue cop astride its yellow frame. "Plpplpplpplp'un," he intoned softly, imitating the sound of a motorcycle as he rolled the toy on the counter top in an imaginary chase of bad guys. "Plpplpplpplp'un," he intoned more loudly.

Suddenly, a large hand slammed his tiny fingers and the toy they held against a glass divider on the counter. The glass broke and sliced the little finger on his right hand. He shrieked as he dropped the motorcycle. Blood oozed from the cut. The powerful steward, who until she saw the blood was smiling for having scored a direct hit, swooned and fell onto the toy counter, collapsing displays and smashing toys beneath her massive frame.

On seeing my brother bleed, I began to cry. The cut was not all that serious, but blood is blood and I was scared of blood. The manager came up and took my brother to the water fountain and set him down on the platform children stood upon to reach the water. He wet his handkerchief and wiped the blood from my brother's finger, telling him everything would be okay.

Meanwhile, somebody lifted the heavy figure from the counter, brought her around, and led her to a back room.

After awhile, my brother's finger quit bleeding. The manager then poured alcohol on the cut. This made my brother howl again. The manager told my brother it wouldn't burn long and it didn't. A clerk produced a Band-Aid and the manager put it over the cut. My brother soon quieted down.

As we started to leave, the huge malevolent form reappeared from the back room. She trudged over to the toy counter and picked up something. She then came to where my brother sat and knelt down beside him. "Here, boy," she said, holding the blood-stained motorcycle out to him. "You want this. You can have it."

My brother gleefully took the toy from her and immediately forgot all about his injury.

We skipped out of the store, passing by the peanut-eating squatters with the brogans and by the screaming street preacher whose voice had grown hoarse. "And I saw the woman drunken with the blood of the saints . . .," he rasped.

"I bet you won't go back in there next Saturday and play with any more of their toys," I said to my brother.

"Why come?" he responded. "She might hit me again and then they'd give me another one of these." He rolled the motorcycle's wheels on the palm of the injured hand. "Plpplpplpplp'un. Plpplpplpplp'un."

His hope to earn another motorcycle through pain and suffering totally disappeared when we returned the following Saturday to find the toy counter no longer defended by the threatening form with the dark glasses but by a younger, more familiar menace. "Don't even look like you want to touch one," our teenage sister snarled at my brother on her first day at work.

PRINCIPLED WRITING

There is an art to writing, it seems
Deforestation measured in reams.
First with a pencil, then with a pen.
Typewriters next. Now computers are in.

But no technology or tricks of the trade
Or formulaed books have one writer made.
It takes something grittier—experiences of life,
Prosaic recountings of conflict and strife.

It takes inspiration, some call it a muse,
To paint word pictures in textual hues;
To make readers laugh or get angry or shiver,
And keep turning pages while crying a river.

It takes dedication, wit, and aplomb
To keep pounding the keys when the words won't come.
It takes great courage and confidence of age
To pour your emotions out on the page.

For some it takes liquor or a cabin in the hills
Or green, hallucinogenic good-writing pills.
But a writer I'll be and as a writer I'll feel
With a six-figure check and a Hollywood deal!

—*Sam Morton*

2-MORT

DEATH AND VELCRO

Carla Damron

My family had gathered under the giant live oak tree that had probably been planted back when dinosaurs roamed the earth. The tree's giant limbs stretched tall above us, clawing at the bright blue sky. A quiet breeze stirred its leaves and played with the hem of my long purple dress.

"Looks like a good day for a funeral," I said.

My uncle Ephraim took the toothpick from his mouth and nodded. He wore his usual faded overalls and bright red Reeboks. I had on a big, floppy hat and the Isadora Duncan scarf I'd purchased at a thrift store for occasions such as this.

My older brother Mordecai let out an audible sigh. He held to the belief that Mom had already had too many funerals. "She just wants to listen to her own eulogy again," he commented.

Mom's funeralizing began twenty years ago when my dad left her. I was nine years old when I watched the clay dust cloud billow up as Dad drove from our trailer for the last time. He'd left a note that said: "Gone for some Salems. Back soon." For a week, Mom sat at the kitchen table waiting for him to return. Then Uncle Ephraim broke the news about the waitress from the Crossroads Diner who'd been spotted loading three suitcases and a brown Shih Tzu in the back of Dad's El Camino.

Mom took the news by taking to bed. For two weeks, she laid on top of Granny's quilt, staring out the window like she expected Dad would change his mind and come back home. Mordecai was left to take care of us, which meant two weeks of peanut butter sandwiches, devil cakes, and Orange Crush sodas.

But things turned around that next Friday morning when Mom burst through the kitchen door. She wore her new Easter dress, white patent leather shoes, and a flowered hat with ribbons flowing off the back. I thought she'd finally toppled over that edge she'd always danced on, but Mom poured herself some coffee and announced: "We're having us a funeral."

"A funeral?" I had asked, trying to remember the phone number to the HELP line.

"Yep. My marriage has died. It was a good marriage before Diner Darlene…" (This was what she called my Dad's mistress.) "…so it deserves a proper send-off. We'll have the funeral at noon. Get on the phone and call your uncle Ephraim."

This began a ritual that became a family tradition. Whenever there was a divorce, a lost job, a loss of something important, we held a funeral. My Aunt Cora threw one when the phone company laid her off. My cousin had one after he totaled his '74 Camaro. This was Mom's fifth; she'd funeralized two divorces, the removal of her gall bladder, and Shannon Faulkner's departure from The Citadel. No one knew why she'd called for today's ritual.

"Are we expecting anyone else?" Mom began, glancing over at me.

I looked up at the road, hoping to see my husband's pick-up. But Bud wasn't coming. Nobody really expected him any more. He'd spent the past two years avoiding me and my family. I fingered my wedding ring, dented on the side during a fight with Bud last year when I learned about his version of "Diner Darlene." I thought. But at least Bud hadn't left me yet, I reminded myself. There was still time for Bud to change.

"Here comes Monroe," Mordecai said, pronouncing his twin's name with an accent on the first syllable. Monroe attended a "special" program for "special" adults where he made thirty dollars a week gluing corrugated boxes. As soon as the yellow minibus pulled into the yard, Monroe flung himself through the sliding side door and ran over to us. He sure wasn't about to miss a good funeral.

"Are we ready?" Mom winked at Monroe, who responded by pulling his favorite piece of Velcro from his pocket. Monroe loved his Velcro, especially the SKROOCH sound it made when he tore the sides apart.

"Ephraim, you may begin." Mom closed her eyes, giving her brother a solemn nod.

Ephraim shot her a perplexed look and began: "Dearly beloved, we are gathered here this day to pay our respects and final goodbyes to…" he turned to Mom. "What are we funeralizing here today, Lucy?"

A big, wide smile spread across Mom's face. She scanned our faces as if waiting for one of us to speak up. Monroe ripped his Velcro so loudly that Mordecai reached over and swatted his hand. I started getting a strange, unsettling sensation in my stomach. Finally, Mom's gaze rested back on me. "Weeza, this funeral is for you."

"Me?" I gasped, the word snagging in my throat.

"Yes you, honey. It's been long overdue. And deep down, I think you know it."

I felt a dozen eyes shift in my direction. I tilted my head to hide my face in the shadow of my hat. That unsettling feeling crawled from my stomach to my chest. My heart thudded so hard against my ribcage I thought it might break free.

"I don't understand," Mordecai said. "I thought you had to call your own funeral."

My mom came over and slid her arm around me. "I called this funeral because Weeza needs our help. This funeral is to pay our last respects to Weeza's marriage."

"But Weeza and Bud aren't divorced," he said.

"He's right, Lucille," Ephraim added with authority, hooking his thumbs around the bib of his overalls. "You can't funeralize a divorce unless the couple asks for it."

Monroe jerked apart his Velcro and stared at one of the pieces, his eyes squinting like they always did when he got confused.

Mom didn't drop a beat. She gave my waist a little squeeze and said, "All right. Weeza, you need to ask for this funeral. Your whole family is here and we're gonna support you no matter what.

"Bud hasn't treated you right since the day you met him. You married him because you were thinking with your glands, not your brain. Bud drinks too much. He can't hold down a job or keep his pants zipped. And furthermore, you don't love him. You just stay married out of stubborn pride. That's no way to live, Weeza."

I swallowed. I looked down at my wedding band, remembering the engagement ring Bud had pawned a year after our wedding. I used to dream that he'd surprise me with an anniversary band. It would twinkle like a star on my finger, a diamond for each year of our marriage. But I had no diamonds now. I had only the dented band.

Monroe came over to me, handing me his dirty, worn Velcro. He pointed to the pocket lint embedded in one of the pieces. "It don't work right," he said. "It don't stick too good when it gets trash in it."

My hand trembled as I looked down at the Velcro, my brother's prize possession.

"It's your call, Weeza," Ephraim said softly.

"Well, she doesn't have to decide right this instant." Mordecai stepped forward, as if he felt a sudden, unprecedented urge to defend me. "This kind of decision takes time."

"This kind of decision takes courage." Mom took my hand and squeezed it.

I looked at the faces around me. Mordecai and Ephraim exchanged awkward glances. Monroe sat down on the ground, plucked a piece of grass and tied it in his shoe lace.

This was my family, I realized. And they would stand beside me no matter what funerals the future might bring.

I drew a deep breath. I slid the wedding ring from my finger and laid it on the ground.

"Looks like a good day for a funeral all right," I whispered.

DO I DARE?

Eating peaches, Mr.Eliot,
is not the question,
nor is wearing
white flannel trousers
my dilemma.

Ah, but…walking
upon the beach
is another story.
The mermaids' song
is so loud that
I am sure
they sing for me.

When I roll my cuffs
or part my hair behind
they only warble louder.

I *might* dare…
if only The Wasteland's
narrow canoe could
be relied upon to appear
when I need to lie
supine in it and escape
the Lovesong.

—*Righton H. McCallum*

UNEASY LIES THE HEAD

Sam Morton

"Drive!" ordered the passenger as he bounced heavily into the back seat of Tony Villella's cab and slammed the door.

"Where to, mister?" Tony asked as he pulled the gear shift lever into drive and eased into traffic. He curiously eyed his passenger through the rearview mirror. Tony was growing evermore cautious. He was only three years away from retirement as a Washington, DC cabbie. *After all*, Tony thought, *this is 1974. A guy can't be too careful, especially with all these nuts you pick up around the White House.*

The passenger had yet to answer, so Tony prodded again, "Any place in particular?"

"I don't care. Just anywhere but this goddamn place," came the clipped reply.

Through the rearview mirror, Tony studied the man in his back seat. His suit was rumpled and he looked as if he'd been up for days. He wore the haggard look of someone whose mind was fraught with trouble. The last thing Tony wanted was to play psychiatrist to some burned out bureaucrat whose problem was probably that his wife caught him screwing his secretary.

Still, the man looked familiar—the deep-set, thoughtful eyes, the large jowls, and the ski-slope nose.

"Hey," said Tony, "has anyone ever told you you look like…"

"I know. I look like Nixon," came the angry reply from the back seat. "I look like Richard Nixon because I *am* Richard Nixon. Richard Millhouse Nixon, President of the US-goddamn-A!"

Tony shifted in his seat nervously. Either he had the most powerful man in the free world in the back seat of his yellow, 1970 Chevrolet Caprice, or he had a dead-ringer psychopath. The prospect of either left his palms damp.

"Look, uh, Mr. Nixon, I don't mean to keep bothering you, but I noticed you're alone. No Secret Service, I mean." Tony repeatedly shifted his eyes from the mirror to the traffic surrounding him. "I don't have much longer before I retire, and, well, it's just that I don't want some trigger-happy G-man blasting me all over the Lincoln Memorial because he thinks I kidnapped the President."

"Don't worry about it, ah…what did you say your name is?"

"Tony, sir."

"Right, Tony…don't worry about it. I've been walking the hallways at the White House for the last two weeks talking to myself. Those guys are beginning to believe I'm losing my gourd. Hell, if they've even noticed I've gone, they probably think I'm standing in the East Wing talking to Thomas Jefferson or something." He gave a bewildered chuckle. "I just had to get out of there," he said, burying his head in his hands.

"I know how it is," Tony said. "Got a wife and three kids. My oldest wants to go to Georgetown. My son, he wants to play soccer. So you'd think what—a pair of shoes and a ball, right? No way, man. It's cleats, knee pads, soccer shirt, soccer shorts, soccer socks. Jeez, it costs a fortune. My wife is always wantin' something new—clothes, furniture, whatever. And I'm out here bustin' my hump six days a week. Sometimes I just gotta get out, too."

Momentarily dumbstruck, Nixon glared incredulously at Tony from the top of his eyes. "Excuse me, Tony, but I am the leader of the free world. I've got people hovering over me twenty-four hours a day, all wanting something.

"I've got Woodward and Bernstein over at The Post trying to burn me a new asshole and every Democrat in America wants to believe I paid a bunch of idiot Cubans to screw up a break-in. I hardly think that compares to financing a new sofa and a goddamn pair of soccer shoes!"

Tony grew quiet, realizing the difficulty of making small talk with the President of the United States. They rode on without speaking for the next half-hour, the only sound breaking the silence an occasional sigh from the back seat.

Tony shook his head, trying to make sense of the situation. The guy looked like Nixon and sounded like Nixon, but was it really him? *Oh well*—he thought as he took a right off the beltway onto 14th Street—*the meter's running and, whoever this guy is, from the looks of his suit, at least he can afford the tab.*

As Tony slowed to a stop at a traffic light on 14th, he heard a gentle rapping on the front passenger glass. He smiled as he looked over to see the outrageously clad drag queen he knew as Gloria Vanderbilt. Gloria had on a bleach-blond wig pulled back in a bun and makeup smeared garishly across her face. Small feathers from her hot-pink boa clung to her neck in the sticky July evening.

Tony leaned over and rolled down the passenger-side window. "Well, hello, Tony-boy. How's business?" Gloria cooed with an exaggerated flourish. Nixon covered his face and slid close to the door.

"Business is good, Gloria. Where've you been? Haven't see you out in the last couple of weeks."

"Well, you know how it is, Tony. You try and try to please your customers, but every now and then one of them comes along who doesn't figure out you're a boy until they're excited enough to drive nails with their little things. The next thing you know, you're in the hospital nursing a couple of ribs. It's a hazard of the business, I guess. But, say, Tony…I could use a few bucks. Could you spot me?"

"Sure," Tony said with resignation as he pulled a ten from his shirt pocket, certain that this would be the last he would see of that money. "I'll catch you next week and you can pay me back, okay?" Tony could see Nixon in the rearview mirror glaring at him as if he'd just set fire to the money and threw in into the gutter.

Gloria stepped back from the cab and swept her arms widely as she made a production of stuffing the money into her over-padded bra. "Tony Villella," she yelled, "you are a prince of a man. I swear it's true. Did you hear that my fellow queer Washingtonians? Tony Villella is a prince of a man." With that she leaned through the passenger window and pulled Tony's face between her gloved hands. She smeared red lipstick all over his cheek as she planted a joyous, but affected kiss.

Tony winced as he slowly pulled from the curb. He used a handkerchief to wipe away the waxy lipstick and chuckled a bit. It had been an unusual night even by Washington standards.

Tony looked into the rearview mirror. Nixon stared mindlessly out the window at the passing neon. "Look, Mr. Nixon, I get off in about 45 minutes. Is there someplace special you need to go?"

Nixon thought for a minute. "No. I guess you can head back. This isn't doing me any good. I'll show you how to get in without getting blasted, as you put it."

As Tony drove, neither said anything. Then Nixon, almost to no one in particular said, "What am I going to do?"

"What's all this talk about impeachment?" Tony asked hesitantly.

"I ought to make the SOB's go through with it. Let them spend dollar after dollar, and let us expose a few skeletons of our own. In the end I'll come out a winner. Hell, I won by a landslide, didn't I?"

"Well, you haven't asked me, but I think you'd come out better by resigning," Tony said.

Nixon's eyes flashed, "No, I didn't ask you Mr. Cab Driver. All I did ask you to do was drive—to get me away from that gaggle of whining little snots who are more concerned about their own political careers than their President.

"And thank you very much, Mr. Cab Driver, because all you did was take me to a den of whores and perverts and make me watch while you implemented your own little social program giving entitlements to a fat, ugly faggot in a dress. Those people bring on their own problems and you support them. Jesus Christ!"

Tony slammed on the brakes. He'd had enough of this pathetic smart mouth and he swung around, for the first time facing the man in the back seat, ready to fire back. "Look here Mr. President, if that's really who you are. You, of all people, ought to know good and damned well about whores and perverts. This city's full of them, most over on Pennsylvania Avenue.

"And talk about bringing on your own problems, pal, well, when you get back to the White House, or wherever it is you live, take a good, long look in the mirror. Now the fare is $37.50. How about pay up, and get the hell out of my cab."

Nixon sat as still and cold as the Lincoln Memorial. Then he tilted his head down. Then only sound was that of the engine idling. "I'm sorry, Tony," he said without looking up. "I really am the President. What were you saying about resigning?"

Tony took a heavy breath as if it was wasted effort, but finally said, "have you ever known an ex-president to have anything but elder statesman status? I mean, everybody looks up to him because, hey, no matter what you did in office, the press and the public always think it's a damn sight better what the poor schmuck who's in there now is doing.

"So retire," Tony said slowly. "Spend your days on the beach or in the mountains, anywhere you want, just get away from it. Hell, in twenty years some baby-boomer will be president and everybody will be so worried that he's gonna give away free acid to the kids, nobody'll care whether you broke into a hotel room or robbed a bank."

For the first time a smile appeared on Nixon's face. "You got a point. Come on. I'm ready to go back."

As Tony pulled up to the South Gate, Nixon opened the door. Before he got out, he leaned over and handed Tony two crisp $100 bills.

"I can't take this," Tony said. "The fare's only $46.75. I'm not a crook."

Nixon smiled, "Neither am I, Tony. Neither am I. But you've got a kid who wants to go to Georgetown."

As he pulled away from the curb and turned off the "For Hire" lamp, Tony looked again in his rearview mirror. In the reflection he saw Nixon wave pensively and then give him the trademark two fingers up. What a strange, screwy night, Tony mused as he rode off into the night.

SUNDAY RITE

Judy Hubbard

Like the Ten Commandments, my family followed a strict unwritten list for practical living.

Brush your teeth before bedtime.

Don't pick your nose in public.

Always pee before you go to church. This edict meant that no matter how dire the need, Mother never let me or my sisters slip out during the worship service.

In my father's big, white, colonial church, with modern plumbing, we easily followed this rule. My grandfather's little churches in Mississippi, however, were another matter.

His (meaning my grandfather, not the Big Father) Baptist church in Weir, Mississippi, defined simplicity: white, plain-fronted, and illuminated with single electric bulbs. The outhouses stood to the right and back, out of smelling range of the sanctuary. One reached them cautiously in small, white Sunday shoes.

The summer I turned seven, my sisters and I spent a month with our grandparents. After Sunday school and before the eleven o'clock service, I always took my obligatory trip.

I walked carefully and stayed alert for snakes as I opened the creaking outhouse door. With the door wide open, I completed the safety check for any lurking critters like a rat or a raccoon or a gorilla.

Satisfied, I located the toilet paper impaled on a peg; and avoiding contact as much as possible, with two fingers I lifted the wooden

322-MORT

cover. Despite the sight and smell, I had to complete my check for snakes.

I evaluated the size of the hole and compared that with the size of my small fanny. This outhouse math produced a danger quotient that guided my subsequent safety procedures. The fear of falling in was ever-present.

With luck, I could perform the necessary relief in a very few gulps of air and limit my exposure to the stench that caused my sunburned nose to wrinkle.

Like a military drill, I moved with efficiency.

Two deep breaths and in. Turn the shaped wooden latch. Lift the dress to avoid soggy petticoats. Turn and face the door. Place hands on either side of hole and lock elbows. Mouth sip of breath.

Lower bottom straight down (sliding could result in splinters.) Balance on front edge of opening. Pee, as fast as possible, while peeking through light slits in door cracks. Watch slivers of rural Mississippi Sunday life. Another shallow sip of air.

Maintaining careful balance, reach for toilet paper. (At times this required two hands and the risk of falling heightened.) Wrap paper around my small hand until it looks like a big Q-tip.

Daub. Daub. Daub. Never wipe with this grade of toilet paper.

Another shallow gulp of air.

Stand and watch the paper as it falls in hole. Gross, but seven-year-old-fascinating.

Do not breathe until wooden lid is down.

Up with the unders, fumble with the door latch and open to deep, full breaths. Fresh air, sunshine, another hour of church.

WET TEVAS
(RIVER SANDALS)

Ankle deep, I stood in the Nantahala
River as a lone green kayak
careened over the falls, flashed
in the sunlight, and shot
point first into the whirlpool at
the bottom of the abyss.
The splash, in juxtaposition
to the water crashing down, created
a split-second rainbow, and diverted
the mind from real danger. In that
awesome moment my son, boat and
all, shot skyward through
the colors…teal streak across
the spectrum, slapped the river, steadied
his kayak in an eddy, and returned
my heart to a steady rhythm. A
double paddle raised in triumph
toward the shore his only
acknowledgment of my presence.
He was twelve.

Snorkling on the surface
I watch the chartreuse streak
which is my youngest son thirty
feet below, swimming into and
out of the shipwreck, coral covered,

fish haunted. A nurse shark circles
more curious than the divers. I am
alone armed only with a mother's
sense and Tevas. The shark surfaces
to nudge the divers' buoy, swims
around the boat, takes playful dashes at
the anchor line and as if to reassure me,
dives once more to traverse the wreck.
"harmless slow ol' things" the
divemasters call them. She is not slow
nor probably harmless…but she is
beautiful as the small sharks begin
to leave her body. Small tiny bundles
like new puppies. We understand each
other, this shark and I. Below us, the
scuba diving men miss the point entirely.

—*Righton H. McCallum*

PASSING STORM

Jeff Koob

Ben stood shivering as he peered into the wailing darkness between two slats in the barn door. The storm was a wall of noise and cascading water that made him weak-kneed with fear. The barn shuddered and creaked all around him as he shook in the furious night, alone, drenched from the rain that the wind drove through the cracks of the trembling, weathered walls.

Many times he had faced terrors in the night, imagining his bedsheets to be armor against all the hurtful things that might lurk in the dark. Now twelve, he was old enough to fall asleep to thunder that had once fed his fears with its DOOM! DOOM! in the near distance. But fears tamed by thousands of nights survived went wild again in the storm. He thought, " If I die, I won't have to be afraid anymore."

Just the day before he had run the stretch between the old barn and the farmhouse easily, without even panting. But tonight the world was ending, and the distance was made vast by the gale winds. Just when he had been poised to dash for the house he was supposed to call home, the beckoning lights had flickered and died. Then the wind had risen like a tide that cuts off two points of land, leaving him stranded. Now he heard the crack of trees breaking outside, the screech of old tin peeling back somewhere overhead, and the inescapable roaring of the wind echoing in his temples. Part of him felt like he had caused the storm—like it had started in his pulse.

He knew he was to blame for the argument that had led to his crazy flight from shelter. Yet there had been no grief, nor even rage, in his heart when he had stormed out into the menacing night. He had felt only pride.

What was I proud of, he asked himself in the dark chaos, and the answer came as quickly as the question. *I felt strong. I got out the door so fast she couldn't stop me.* But now death was closer than he had ever imagined it to be, and he was no longer strong. Nothing in his life had prepared him for this night.

The wind hammered at the creaking barn door Ben cowered behind, threatening to snap the old wood around the center bolt, driving him back deeper into the pitch darkness of the barn. His heart pounded in counterpoint to the rhythms of destruction outside. The storm blew all of the triumph out of his defiance, leaving him at the mercy of a world whose terrors he had only just begun to fathom. The nearby shelter of Aunt Rachael's orderly household seemed a world away.

In the sullen evening, when the hurricane was only a word on the TV news, Ben had tried to punish Aunt Rachael for her strictness.

Preoccupied with preparations for the coming storm, she ignored his loud silence until well past their early supper. He lay on his bed in a clutter of rumpled clothes and unopened schoolbooks, staring up at the ceiling when she burst into his room without knocking.

"I told you an hour ago to fill up those milk jugs with water. Why haven't you done it?"

"Didn't feel like it. Besides, the news said the hurricane is gonna strike south of here, Savannah maybe."

"I didn't ask you if you felt like it, young man; I said *do* it! The TV just said the storm is heading in our direction again. On your feet, *now*!"

Ben sat up and swung his feet over the side of the bed. He could tell that his aunt was angry, at the end of her tether, so he only defied her with his eyes. "Why can't Daryl do it? I'm doing my homework."

She ignored his lie. "He's a little boy! He's already in bed." She closed her eyes for a moment and sighed. "You'd think, with your uncle in the hospital, you'd at least *try* to be the man of the house. This is going to be a big storm, and I need your help. I've got more important things to do than argue with you, so get to it!"

Aunt Rachael turned and left the room. Feeling a little guilty, Ben got up and followed her downstairs to the kitchen. She had run out of tape for the windows and rummaged around for more in the cupboard as he started filling the jugs at the sink. He watched her dart around the room, a diminutive dynamo. He was almost ready to call a truce, when she said the wrong thing.

"You know," she said, pausing in her inspection of her husband's box of odds and ends for extra tape, "when we took you in, I thought you might even be grateful. If it weren't for us you'd be in another foster home now. You have your own room here, and you don't lack for anything. We don't ask much of you, but—"

"Maybe I'd rather be in a foster home! You never let me do anything!"

"Young man, you lost your privileges because you were suspended from school for three days, so don't you go feeling sorry for yourself."

Ben whirled and faced her. "You don't really care about me! You just took Daryl and me so you could get Momma's welfare check."

Aunt Rachael looked like she had been slapped, and Ben immediately regretted what he had said. She and Uncle Jim had been kinder to him and had given him more than any foster parents, or even his mother, ever had. They just had so many rules.

Aunt Rachael's voice had an edge to it. "If your mother cared about you as much as we do, you wouldn't have been taken away from her. She only cared about her drugs and her—"

"Don't you talk about my momma! At least she let me do

things. If I run away I know right where to find her, and you'll never see me again!"

"Fine. You don't like it here, I'll just call the social worker tomorrow and we can put you back in the Boys' Home again. If we can't teach you that everybody's got to follow *some* rules, maybe somebody else can."

Ben felt so full of hurt and anger he thought he would explode. There was only one thing to do: run. He ran to the door and flung it open, backing his way out the screen door and onto the porch.

"I hate you!" he yelled. Rain filled the air, and the wind rose in the dark.

"No!" Aunt Rachael stood silhouetted in the doorway, helpless. "Get back in, please! There's a bad storm coming; you could be killed. Don't be stupid!"

Ben felt more powerful with every backward step into the night. There was something intoxicating in the wind. "So what if I die? Who cares?" he shouted at the house.

"Please come back, Ben! I didn't mean it about the Boys' Home."

"I don't need you!" The rain felt cool on his skin as he ran from the light toward the shelter of the barn. He told himself how sorry she would be if he died, but he was not really afraid.

He knew he would go back to the house after he cooled down. By the time he reached the barn he had convinced himself he was a man.

In the darkness Ben could barely see his own hands, even after all this time in the barn. Then he heard the sound of his own sobbing and suddenly realized that the winds had subsided. He stumbled forward to peer out between the slats. He thought he could make out the silhouette of the farmhouse in the gloom. He stopped crying.

He was in the eye of the storm.

Before he knew what he was doing he threw back the bolt,

pushed through the heavy doors, and ran out into the still center of the vast cyclone. The mud sucked at his feet, slowing him as he splashed his way across the farmyard. The sight of stars overhead amazed him, as if he were seeing them for the first time. And then the farmhouse loomed before him, dark and solid.

He clumped up the steps onto the porch, guided by a sliver of light beneath the kitchen door. The familiar squeak of the screen door greeted him. The kitchen door was unlocked.

He stumbled over the threshold into dim, flickering light.

Aunt Rachael stood in the door to the hallway, illuminated by a lantern held at shoulder height. Daryl clung to her other hand and gaped at his big brother, who stood muddy and dripping in the spotless kitchen. Nobody said anything, but Aunt Rachael wept as she released Daryl's hand, ducked back into the hallway and re-entered the room with a blanket. Placing the lantern on the kitchen table, she unfolded the blanket and handed it to Ben. When he had draped it over his shoulders, she threw her arms around him in a fierce hug.

"I'm so glad you're home," she sobbed. Shivering, Ben hugged her back as never before.

He awoke in the bright morning from a dream in which he had seen the hand of God, but the dream images blurred into a flood of memories from the night before. He was in his own bed, in his own room. Leaning over to the bedside table, he tried to switch on the lamp, to see if they had power. All he got was a click. He rose and went to the window.

Most of the fence lay in ruins. Branches and debris littered a mud flat that had been a farm field the day before. Puddles the size of small ponds splotched the desolate landscape all the way to a strange, new horizon of fallen and sundered trees. The barn roof had blown away and two adjacent walls leaned in at crazy angles.

He dressed and ran downstairs. In the kitchen Aunt Rachael had fixed a cold breakfast. Daryl sat at the table playing with his cereal, jabbering away. "I don't have to go to kindygarden today," he announced.

"Is it okay if I go out and look around?" Ben asked. He thought of the three of them huddled together in the space under the stairs, only hours ago, as the storm renewed its fury. He remembered the terror and the prayers during the worst of it, and the relieved laughter they had shared after the storm had passed.

"Have some breakfast first. The driveway's blocked, and the radio says the power's out all over the county. We caught the worst of the hurricane. The phone still works, so your uncle knows we're safe."

"I'm not hungry. Please? I've never seen anything like this. I'll be back soon."

"Well, at least drink some milk, before it sours." Aunt Rachael poured a glass full and handed it to Ben. "You had me scared sick last night, you know."

"I know. It was a dumb thing to do." He drained the glass and handed it back. "I don't really want to go live somewhere else."

He barely avoided a hug on his way to the door. Outside, he slogged through a sea of mud, in awe of the devastation all around him. The big pecan tree by the garden shed lay on its side, roots torn from the earth. Hardly a pine tree in sight still stood tall or bore a crown of green, and nothing looked quite familiar. Caught up in a frenzy of discovery, he explored the transformed landscape and wondered, *"Did God do this?"*

He saw a butterfly flutter up from a pile of wreckage, and marveled that such a fragile thing could have survived the hurricane. Then, remembering his promise to return soon, he turned around and was immediately struck by the sight of the farmhouse. It was the only structure in sight left intact. Sensing storms yet to come in the morning breeze, he headed back toward home.

A QUESTION

Tell
me
this:
Why
is it
that
those
who oppose abortion
favor
capital   punishment
while   those
who   favor
abortion   oppose
capital   punishment?
*   *

—*Bert Goolsby*

CORA'S KARMA

Judy Hubbard

The truth is, I exist only by the grace of God and my grandmother's magnificent nose. Or so I have always been told.

* * *

For as long as I can remember, a very plain looking cabinet in my parents' living room has called to me, beckoning me to a realm where time moves backward.

In this magic place, years vanished. In hundreds of small miracles, I saw the old grow young and beautiful, the long dead live again, and my parents become children.

There, in the flat wonderland of my family's photographs, cloistered in the walnut cabinet.

My journey always started with a crumbling, dark brown leather album, bound with a black silk cord and adorned with slanting letters that spelled "Photographs." The heavy, earthy scent of the album's black pages initiated my time travel.

Four tiny black paper corners held each photo in place; and below many of the snapshots, my mother's upright handwriting identified names and places. Other photographs stood unmarked like mysteries or unfinished thoughts.

The photos preserved fragments of stories—faces, landscapes, my parents' courtship and wedding, holidays, vacations and births.

Moments saved for me by the camera.

One photo showed three people on a wide light sand beach.

My father, lean, young, clad only in bathing trunks, squints into the bright Florida sunlight. My older sister, Gwen, stands tiny, swathed in a hooded white terrycloth robe. My grandmother sits on the sand, her legs tucked to one side. She looks back over her shoulder toward my mother, who holds the camera.

I knew this snapshot's story. The year is 1945. My grandmother, Cora Buckner Knight, vacations with her son's family at Daytona Beach, Florida. Grandmother, sixty-seven years old, wears her first bathing suit, bought for this occasion.

The photo captures three generations—mother, son, and granddaughter, each life balanced on the one before.

* * *

I breathe in the scent of the photo album, close my eyes, and time shifts. The year is 1890, and my grandmother is a child growing up in a small Kentucky town.

"Cora! Cora, come here, please," Dolie Buckner called to her daughter.

Lanky Cora Buckner marked her place and reluctantly snapped the book closed. As she stood, her ankles poked out from beneath the dark blue skirt, its hem having been let out twice that year already. Glancing in the mirror above the cherry chest of drawers, she frowned at how her dark eyebrows dominated her pale, thin face. *Doesn't anyone else live in this house but me?* she fumed.

"Cora, please run this note over to Mrs. Baker. It's about the women's meeting tomorrow. We've got to change the time. You don't mind, do you dear?" Dolie implored.

As a matter of fact, Cora resented anything that took her away from her world of books, but she acquiesced. If she hurried she could be reading again in ten minutes, provided that Mrs. Baker didn't start with her endless questions.

At full speed, Cora flew out the back door and down the steps. In five long strides she reached the picket fence and halted.

There, not twenty yards away, her older brother, Malcolm, stood on the edge of the vegetable garden. His shirt clung to his back, moist from the exertion on a warm April afternoon. Sunlight glinted off the bright metal of the hoe he swung, and the blade produced a "shesh" sound as it sliced through the dark, rich soil.

Cora shrank back and watched her brother's rhythmic movements. He seemed mesmerized by the cadence and completely unaware of her nearness.

The four year gap between Cora's twelve and Malcolm's sixteen years created a tender attachment expressed in teasing and pranks. Malcolm's preoccupation now offered Cora an irresistible opportunity as she picked her way along the fence shielded with budding lilac bushes.

Silently she slipped through the gate and waited. As Malcolm began his next swing, she crept forward and slipped in behind him. As he once again raised the hoe, Cora reached out and tickled his sides, an irrepressible giggle rising in her throat.

In reflex, Malcolm jerked his arms, and the hoe flew backwards. Cora looked up in the same instant that the sharp blade filled her field of vision.

"Pshaw!" Malcolm reacted to the ambush.

There had been no one nearby; but even without looking, he understood. "Cora!" he laughed in playful anger as he whirled around. "Cora?" but this time his voice had flattened. "Cora!" and the sound of horror filled her name.

Something is terribly wrong, Cora thought through a numbing fog.

Her vision blurred and blood gushed warm and crimson from somewhere. Curiously Cora's fingers explored her face—first chin, then mouth and finally, nose. Her nose, numbed by a gash. Her nose, which now hung barely attached at the base of her nostrils. Another quarter of an inch deeper and it would have been severed from her face.

And, with this realization, Cora wisely fainted dead away.

Malcolm cried out not a word, but an expulsion of rage and

denial. Inside his house and throughout the neighborhood, the noise reverberated. It was the kind of sound that chills a mother's heart, and when Dolie Buckner heard, she came running.

Malcolm gasped and stammered out the words, "I-I-I don't know what happened! I-I-I never saw her."

Kneeling down and stifling waves of nausea, a terrified mother called to her daughter, but Cora did not move. Dolie Buckner fought her panic as she pulled a white handkerchief from her blue gingham apron's pocket. With gritted teeth, she repositioned Cora's nose and applied pressure as the handkerchief's lace turned scarlet.

Malcolm stood close by, pale and wobbling in his boots.

"Go get your papa. Tell him to come home fast," Dolie commanded her son.

Malcolm ran for Cora's life, not knowing if she lay drowning in her own blood. He ran for his own life, trying to distance himself from the hoe which now lay unseen among the spring plantings.

Cora and Malcolm's father, Dr. Joseph Buckner, was an irascible autocrat. Twenty five years earlier in the Civil War, a wayward musket ball had destroyed his left arm and his ability to perform surgery. Now he bitterly described his practice as "pill-pushing," but he could manage a one-handed delivery of babies and simple emergency procedures in dire circumstances.

Finding his father at his office, Malcolm sketched in what little he understood of how the accident had happened. Each word burned in his throat like venom.

"Doc" Buckner roared into action, grabbing his black bag as he bolted out the office door. By the time he and Malcolm reached home, neighbors had carried the unconscious Cora into the house.

Most days Dolie Buckner accepted her much older husband's tyranny but not this day. Through a veil of near hysteria she demanded, "Joseph, Cora can't live this way. You have to fix this!"

Doc Buckner listened and understood too well. Festering wounds that poisoned and killed countless young rebel soldiers still haunted his dreams. He had operated on young soldiers who

322-MORT

lost arms, legs, eyes and ears. He had witnessed their agony of waking to bandages and stumps.

Despite his now one-handedness, Doc continued to think like a surgeon. Since his medical training at Vanderbilt he had followed scientific breakthroughs and applied them to his small town practice.

Ten years earlier Cora would have been damned to life as a noseless freak, if she lived at all. But only in the previous decade Sir Joseph Lister had revolutionized surgery with his understanding of infection. Doc recalled how carelessly he had wiped his hands, sometimes on the grass, to remove the blood between wartime surgeries. No wonder so many died.

Now the same domineering personality that often intimidated Cora came forth as her dogged champion. With Doc as the commander, the family and neighbors became a unit of soldiers preparing for battle. Boiling hot water sterilized the needles, sutures and bandages. Clean sheets covered the kitchen table which would be the operating site. From the icehouse neighbors fetched precious ice to moderate pain and swelling. From his bag Doc took the purple antiseptic, potassium permanganate, commonly called gentian violet. No one said aloud the word "gangrene."

If the wound had been in another location, Doc could have used ether as an anesthetic, but the wound through the nasal passages precluded its use. Cora's unconscious state was her only shelter from the pain.

So, with his right hand and left stump, Doc Buckner began. Neighbors immobilized Cora's head, shoulders and arms while Dolie held the nose in position. As best he could, Doc Buckner cleaned and disinfected the wound with soapy water and then the gentian violet. Luckily for Cora, the hoe had been brand new, and the wound was deep but well defined.

Dolie tried not to look each time the short fine needle pierced her daughter's ghostly pale skin. Cora's eyes remained closed and she made no sound, but her clinched lips quivered with each piercing of the needle. One tiny black stitch at a time, Cora's "Papa" reattached her nose.

Over the next few days time dragged cruelly as Cora drifted in and out of reality. Each minute seemed glued one to the next. When Cora woke, her hand would touch her bandages and she would remember.

The calamity shattered Dolie Buckner's rationality. To her, Cora's life seemed ruined—never to marry, never to have children of her own, never to be lovely again. Dolie watched her son Malcolm's vigor and wit evaporate into guilt and remorse. She watched her younger daughter, Lena, escape into her drawings. Overwhelmed, Dolie wept to release the pain her heart could not contain.

Dr. Buckner raged. He yelled at everything—the dog, his horse, the weather, and his late supper. He stomped through the house and flung down his hat and coat. He grumbled and growled, gesturing wildly with his stump of an arm.

Finally, after agonizing days of waiting, Cora began to rouse. Although swelling, bruising and the antiseptic turned much of her face dark and purple, no infection developed and her nose grew warm to the touch. It even began to itch.

Each day Malcolm faced endless, unanswerable questions about Cora as he waited on customers at the family's drygoods store.

"How's your little sister?"

"What does she look like?"

"Is it really growing back?"

"Bet you feel just awful."

The talk cut as sharply as the hoe.

Dolie Buckner could not bear for anyone to see Cora's distorted face while it healed. When visitors came, some sincere, some curious, she turned them away with polite words like, "Cora's resting," or "Why don't you write Cora a note?" If visitors managed to come inside, Dolie hid Cora in the closet.

The closet was humiliating for Cora, but she understood. Her mother, beyond reason, was only trying to protect both of her children. Cora did look frightening—a bit like Mary Shelley's Frankenstein character, and it had been her own fault, not Malcolm's. It never occurred to her to blame Malcolm.

Although Cora agreed to the hiding, all the while she plotted her escape. There in the dark closet among the coats, a metamorphosis began. Cora, cocooned away from the world, began to distance herself from the tragedy. Neither her mother's hysteria nor her father's tirades seemed right to this gawky, forthright girl-woman. She would find her own way back.

Refusing to be cast as the Buckner's unfortunate daughter, Cora resorted to making wisecracks about her injury. And as she gingerly began to smile again, being careful not to wrinkle her nose, the pall of the crisis lifted.

Determined, Cora reentered the world. She dressed in her favorite blue clothes and took extra care with her long braided blond hair. She tried to move as if she were beautiful, and, in time, she almost would be.

She embraced imperfect solutions, like the reddened scar that appeared across the bridge of her nose. Where her nose had once been straight, the end now turned up at a slightly askew angle, and she used this as evidence in her lively retelling of her War of the Tickle. Like her father, she had been caught in the line of fire. Like him, she would always carry scars; but her scarring would only be skin-deep.

* * *

I open my eyes and look down at the black album page and the photo braced by four tiny black corners.

I see my grandmother sitting on the beach with her son whom she named for her brother. Like his uncle, my father Malcolm, is dreadfully ticklish.

The camera records Cora smiling beside her teetering sand castle at the edge of the surf. A red bathing cap covers her long gray braided hair. I can barely see the scar on her magnificent, slightly turned-up nose.

TIME TO FIND A LOVER

She was sitting at the bar
Glassy eyed and smiling
It was late and she'd come early
She'd been there way too long
Her Thursday morning hairdo
Was falling down around her
Her dreams and plans and chances
Like the night were almost gone.

The night was fading quicker
Than the magic in the liquor
And the pain of sitting there alone
Was more than she could take.
Time to put her pride aside
And find someone to leave with
Feeling bad or feeling lonely
The only choice she gets to make

Pride and better judgement—
No match for drunk and lonely
They're only an excuse to use
When all she gets is stoned
And if she gets to make a choice
Then feeling bad tomorrow
Will be easier to handle
Than to face tonight alone.

Time to find a lover
A companion, friend, or brother
Another soul to share the cold
And keep the pain away
Keep the pain away until
Tomorrow if it only will
Lonely makes the morning feel
A million years away.

—*John Bolin*

CALIFORNIA

John Bolin

Lord God Almighty it was hot and it had been hot for what seemed like an eternity. South Carolina in July doesn't get any better than miserable. The closest thing to dying and going to hell is being held hostage on a truck farm and being forced to pick butter beans on a Wednesday afternoon in the July heat. It must have been 110 degrees and there was not a breath of air moving on the earth's surface. My spine was permanently warped from picking. I was crippled for life because of them Goddamn butter beans.

We'd been picking butter beans for three straight days and we were just about through the first picking. You don't just pick butter beans once, you know. You pick the sons-of-bitches all summer long. The butter bean is like kudzu with fruit. Had I not been able to see the end of the last row—and ultimately an end to this misery and madness—I had decided to find a low limb on a tall tree so I could beg some bed sheets, make a rope and hang myself. I was hot, tired, hurting, desperate, and mad.

Picking butter beans can make you crazy. Stooped over for days at a time, dragging a tin tub full of beans behind you, breathing dust and bug poison, slapping gnats, sweat dripping off your chin and your elbows and the sun frying the back of your neck. It will make you crazy as hell.

It'll make you crazy and it will make you mean, too. Most of the mass murderers in this country I bet spent serious time in the bean fields of the South. I suspect most of the chain saw and ax murder plots were incubated in some dumb son of a bitch's sun fried brain in the middle of a bean field south of the Mason-Dixon. There's no doubt in my mind.

Butter beans was not my idea. My stepfather, Tom Martin, had gotten a revelation during the winter of 1956 and he thought there might be significant money made selling produce to the grocery stores up town. We had a little property—three or four acres—and he had some cheap labor—mainly me and my brother—so he thought he'd match up the best parts of both, give us something to keep us occupied during the summer and maybe make a little extra spending money to boot.

Tomatoes and butter beans and squash and okra was Tom Martin's idea of a truck farm. He got really carried away on the butter beans though and by the time we finished planting, we had almost an acre. An acre of butter beans! Do you have any idea how many butter beans can be produced on an acre? You could probably feed China on an acre of butter beans.

The first morning we went out to pick butter beans, my brother and I each took a number three tin tub, or "wash tub" as we called them, to pick in. Number three wash tubs are round, gray galvanized tin tubs with handles on the sides that clanged like cow bells when you hauled them around—large enough to take a bath in.

I started picking on the first row of butter beans and by the time I got a third of the way to the end of the first row, I had picked my number three tin tub full. Full! Running over the edge, falling out on the ground, slap-ass full. I quickly calculated that at three tubs full to the row would eventually produce about 90 tubs of butter beans. Mind boggling!

When we came in for dinner—today we call it lunch—we had picked through the first 15 rows and we had about 40 tubs of butter beans. If I could have gotten my hands on a pistol, I would have shot Tom Martin. Then I would have shot myself.

We picked and shelled and dried and froze and canned and sold and hauled and gave away butter beans nearly all that summer. Every day of July, we picked and shelled butter beans. Every day except Sundays. We went to church on Sundays so we could tell God how grateful we were to be allowed to labor in his vineyards. I was grateful. I was so grateful at the prospect of getting up every morning and walking down past the barn and looking at that green expanse of butter beans that I couldn't sleep at night. We were bean zombies.

If I thought I could have cut a deal with the Devil concerning a reprieve from those bean fields, I'd have a pitchfork, a long tail, and horns today.

It was about two o'clock and we had been picking since daylight and the end was nowhere in sight. Kenny and I were picking side by side. Picking and grunting. It was 100 degrees—too hot to talk. On our way back to the field after dinner, Kenny had picked two or three big ripe Big Boy tomatoes and had put them in his tub. These Big Boys were about the size of softballs and he was either going to eat them or throw them—depending on how the afternoon went. I looked up when I heard a car coming down the road that ran past our property.

"Looks like ol 'Whizzer Foster's car," I said.

Whizzer Foster lived down the road and around the curve from my house. I never knew where the name "Whizzer" came from but it didn't sound at all strange to me until I grew up and moved away.

"There's something wrong with that old fart." Kenny never liked Whizzer.

"What do you mean?" I asked.

"Something about him just gives me the creeps. He moves like a Goddamn snake."

Come to think of it, Whizzer did kinda remind you of a snake. Whizzer was maybe fifty years old, more than six feet tall but I bet he didn't weighed 130 pounds. He had narrow shoulders, little beady eyes, translucent eyelids with bright red spider veins and a real bony face. He had kind of a slick, fluid motion when he moved and he did everything at about the same deliberate speed. Whizzer would be sitting in one of the straight backs at old man Smith's store and he'd say something like, "Better be gittin on home. See you boys later." Then he'd uncoil and kinda slide out the door. No noise—no commotion. Kenny said he thought Whizzer could unhinge his jaw.

What Kenny really hated about Whizzer was that Whizzer was a toucher. He'd come up on you from behind and slide one of those long tentacle arms of his across your shoulders and pinch the back of your neck or tweak your ear. God, his hands were always cold. Cold like a dead man's. Kenny said he thought Whizzer liked boys but I didn't know what that meant until I got to the sixth grade.

"Watch me hit the son-of-a-bitch with this tomato," Kenny said as Whizzer came rolling down the road.

"You won't get close." I didn't think he had a chance.

When Whizzer saw Kenny and me, he stuck his head out the window to give us a big smile and Kenny fired a perfect strike with that ripe Big Boy.

The tomato missed Whizzer's head by a whisker, sailed past his face and exploded against the inside of the passenger side window. It scared him so bad that he jerked the steering wheel to the right, jumped the ditch and plowed across Ronnie George's mama's front yard. Crystal George, Ronnie's mama, was scouring the front porch when it happened. She panicked when Whizzer's Ford flew across her yard, plowed through her marigolds and nearly knocking her front steps down. When Crystal looked at the passenger side window of Whizzer's Ford, all she could see was a window full of red tomato pulp.

"God almighty, God almighty. Whizzer Foster's been shot through the head. His brains is all over the car." And with that, she fainted.

Crystal was a big girl and when she fainted, she fell in a deck chair on the porch. It withstood the initial impact but it couldn't sustain her settling weight. When she flopped in the chair, it slammed shut like a trap.

"Sorry about your car, Mr. Whizzer," Tom said. "It don't seem to be hurt none other than the tomato on the seats. I can't say the same for Crystal's flower bed though. Kenny and John will clean up your car just as soon as I whip their asses."

"I do hate to see them boys get a whippin," said Whizzer. "But they nearly scared Crystal George to death. I thought we never would get her breathing right. Throwing things at cars just ain't right. They're pretty good boys but you just can't allow them to throw things at automobiles."

"Right after I beat their asses," Tom huffed.

"I would like some of those butter beans though. They do look pretty. You think you could spare a peck or two?"

"Boys," Tom yelled at us, "Get something to put some of them beans in and put them in Mr. Whizzer's car."

Tom Martin and Whizzer walked up toward the house and Kenny and I started looking around for something to put some beans in.

"I'll give the son of a bitch some butter beans." A storm began to brew in Kenny.

He picked up a number three tin tub full of beans and dumped fifty pounds of beans in the back floor seat of Whizzer's Ford. Ten minutes and ten or twelve tubs later, butter beans were spilling out of every window of Whizzer's Ford.

Kenny went around front where Tom and Whizzer were sitting on the front porch. He had a rod and reel in one hand and a tackle box in the other.

"I'm going to Wesson's lake to fish for catfish and I'm going to stay all night. I ain't hungry and I don't want no supper. We put some butter beans in Mr. Whizzer's car. See you tomorrow."

He said it so fast and with such a deliberate look on his face that I don't think Tom wanted to challenge him. Kenny left and didn't come back till the next day. Butter beans will make you bold like that sometimes.

Late that afternoon the weather took a change and the strangest thing happened. We had the damnedest windstorm you have ever in your life seen. It had been over a hundred degrees every day for the past two weeks. Even the ground was hot so I guess it was nature's way of cooling things off. The wind started blowing real hard about lunchtime—before we got into the tomato-throwing incident—and by three o'clock, it was really howling. The sky got real black and there were clouds not more that a hundred feet high racing by like flying boxcars.

John Ervin, who lived right across the road, came over and beat on my back door.

"Get your bicycle. The wind will blow you down the road." John Ervin was excited.

And he was right. The wind was blowing about forty miles an hour right down the road that ran in front of our house. You could get out in the road with your back to the wind and it would literally push you along.

"God damn, what if we made us a sail. We could sail our bicycles all over the place. Just like sailing a boat. Shit, it'll be just like California."

Everything slick or new or extreme or radical was "just like California" to John Ervin. He'd seen a sailplane and a surfboard on a California Chamber of Commerce poster at the post office and he was forever smitten. To John Ervin, California was the "land of all things beautiful."

I got a big bed sheet from my mama's linen closet and sneaked it out to the barn. We quickly nailed together a frame maybe six feet by four feet and tacked the bed sheet to the frame. Getting the sail to stay on the bicycle was a little more difficult.

"I've got it." John Ervin reached for the Sears stick welder on the workbench. It was a little 110-volt arc welder that we used to fix broken garden equipment. He turned the welder up to sixty amps, stuck in a mild steel welding rod and laid a six foot piece of galvanized water pipe up against the down tube of his twenty four inch Western Flyer bicycle—and welded it on.

"That ought to hold," he said.

We stuck a piece of angle iron on the top of the water pipe, forming a kind of crude "T" and we were ready to mount the sail. We secured the sail to the frame with some wire hangers and stabilized the whole thing with bailing wire. We were ready to go. Meanwhile, the wind was howling.

We couldn't move the bicycle against the wind when we pushed it outside. The sail did exactly what it was supposed to do. The wind was blowing about fifty miles an hour by now and there was no way we were going to push the bike against it.

"We'll have to carry it sideways," John Ervin yelled over the wind.

With me on one end and John Ervin on the other, we carried the bicycle and sail sideways all the way to Cross Eyed Peter Johnson's house almost a half-mile straight up from my house. Augusta Road might well have been a drag strip from Peter's house to mine—but then Augusta Road did a ninety-degree turn down the hill to the Evers' house. Cross-eyed Peter came out of his house to see what we were doing.

"Let me ride it first,'" yelled Peter. You could barely hear him over of the wind. Peter was about thirty pounds lighter than either me or John Ervin.

"OK! It will take both of us to hold it against the wind," John Ervin yelled at me.

I had one side of the sail and John Ervin had the other when Peter got on the bike.

"Let her go!" yelled Peter. "Let her go!" And that's what we did.

The bike wobbled for a second before it began to roll straight. John Ervin and I ran along side Peter until the bike began to really pick up speed. By the time Peter got a quarter of the way down Augusta Road, he was going probably twenty miles an hour. A big wind shear grabbed him and it looked like a rocket kicked in. The wind got in that sail and launched him down the road. The force of the wind negated any attempt to steer. Peter just hung on.

By the time Peter got two thirds of the way down the road, he was going about forty miles an hour. By the time he hit the curve, I bet he was going fifty or sixty. Do you know how fast fifty or sixty miles an hour is on a twenty-four inch bicycle? John Ervin's sister said she saw Peter's face when the wind really got him. She said all she could see was his eyes. She said they were as big a dinner plates and he was screaming like a scalded cat.

Peter did all right as long as the road went straight. The curve's what really did him in. He didn't know he couldn't turn the handlebars with all that wind behind him. He could turn the handlebars all he wanted to but it didn't have any effect on the direction of the bicycle. The road curved but with the force of all that wind, the bike went straight. Straight across the ditch and through a stand of ten year old pine trees.

Linda Cupps saw it all and she said the first thing Peter hit was a skinny pine tree about eight feet off the ground. That's probably what saved his life. Had he hit one of the big trees a solid lick, it would have killed him outright. Up that high, he was in the limbs and that kinda slowed him down. The second and third trees he hit though, he hit pretty solid. Linda said he looked kinda like a Superman rag doll flying through the air. The impact ripped off the sail, ripped off the front wheel of the bicycle and knocked a couple of big knots on Peter's head. Knocked out a couple of teeth and broke his collarbone, too. When we got to him, I thought he was dead. He didn't breath for a long time.

By the time we got the bike back together and the sail back on, the wind had died down and it had started to rain. We never got to bicycle sail again. Nobody but Peter every knew what going to California really felt like. He knew but he wouldn't talk about it.

Me and John Ervin were heading back to the house when I spied Tom Martin and Whizzer turning the corner to go round back of the house where Whizzer's car was parked.

"Damn, they've found the butter beans," I said.

"I'll beat they're asses. Yes, by damn it, I'll beat they're asses. Can't turn my back. Where are they? Where are they? I'm going to beat them to death." Tom Martin had gone off his nut.

"Goddamn, he's pissed off." John Ervin ducked behind a feed barrel.

"Them god damn butter beans are going to get one of us killed before it's over with." I hid behind John Ervin.

We picked through the beans for the last time the first week in August. After we picked through the last time, Kenny and I went back—and with our bare hands—pulled up every single butter bean plant and piled them up right in the middle of the field. The pile was big as a school bus.

We let them cook in the August sun for about two weeks and then we poured kerosene on them and set them on fire. They burned all night. It was the most pleasant night I ever remember. Red butter bean sparks lit up the moonless night. I know how the Russian soldiers must have felt when they watched Berlin burn.

I started the sixth grade two weeks later and I remember I still had chlorophyll stain under my thumbnails.

It was early September, 1956.

322-MORT

CHANGE

Change
The only thing that is constant,
It sits like a weight on your chest.
A heavy rock, longing to be lifted, flung away,
Releasing the energy underneath,
Requiring superhuman strength.
Placed just under the breastbone,
Slightly to the right.
The flesh burns from its weight,
Cowers in its enormity,
Waiting to be drug, flung, exploded,
Holding the flesh in.
Rise up.
Fling it.
Burst it.
Shatter it.
Leave it.
Go on!
Live!

—Ann Furr

BEACH MEMORIES

Ann Furr

When Louise divorced, it seemed like everything would be better if she could just move to the beach. With friends and family pushing and pulling, she packed a big U-Haul truck and drove with the boys to the beach that she had loved since childhood, driving out of her old life and into a new, exciting one. It had been a good idea. At the beach she wouldn't have to worry about coming face to face with *her* at any moment at the gas station or in the grocery store. She didn't have to go out every day and face her old friends, whose mournful eyes and voices were like a choir singing a funeral dirge. She hated the condescending looks and the kindnesses generally reserved for the terminally ill. Overnight, the pleasant street and house where her children had been brought up had turned into a mausoleum. The heavy salt-filled air and the isolation was the tonic she needed to begin to feel normal again.

Now, five years later, her life had fallen back into the dry routine of sameness, this time beach sameness. Never mind that she lived two rows back from the water's edge on a palm covered barrier island; her life had become as dull and humdrum as anyone else's. People just didn't seem to grasp that part of the equation. They thought that because you live at the beach your life must be constantly exciting—filled with beach picnics and wild gyrations to beach music.

But Louise knew the truth. She heard the alarm blare out its command each morning. She pulled herself out of tortuous sleep and into the bathroom to check her face for new wrinkles and sags.

She roused the kids, got them dressed, pushed the pop tarts down into the toaster, loaded the boys into the old station wagon, dropped them off at the baby-sitters and headed into the city for her day in the harness. Over and over, day after day she pictured herself as a porter, hunched forward, carrying a load of someone else's things.

Peter's annual visit was always both exhilarating and exasperating. She and Peter had been best friends since high school. She had married, had kids, divorced, moved to the beach. Peter had moved to New York, flung himself into city life and become a pulp fiction writer. He liked to work and drink all night, go to bed in the morning and rise for the day about three in the afternoon after nine good hours of rest. He also liked to come South once a year for two weeks with Louise, his oldest and dearest friend. His visit put two rows of brightly colored blocks on the otherwise gray squares that marked the passing of time on her wall calendar.

This was the fourth day of his annual visit, and for the fourth time Louise stopped at the Island Liquor Store on her way home for a fifth of Jack Daniel's.

The clerk looked at her through narrowed eyes. "Lady, it sure ain't none of my business, but are these all for you? I mean you're a nice lady and all and I hate to think of you finishin' one of these off every night."

"Nah," she laughed. "It's for my house guest. He's a famous writer from New York City. You know how they are. I drink a little white wine myself, but none of this hard stuff."

She hadn't stopped at the liquor store for Peter but three or four times during last year's visit, Louise remembered. Maybe Peter's liver needed a vacation. Still Peter was almost the perfect house guest as you didn't have to worry about entertaining him all day, since he was asleep. He loved her boys and they him, and he had ample energy for entertaining them between daycare and bedtime. After they were tucked in, he cooked one of his famous meals for the two of them. He favored fresh seafood, either things he pulled from the briny deep or from the trendy seafood market down the block, accompanied by fresh vegetables from her back-yard garden. He was a great cook and an unending supply of original recipes popped out of his head.

The two of them would savor the nightly feast and ruminate for hours. Louise would tumble into bed and Peter would watch late night TV or haul out his laptop to work on his latest thriller. He claimed that the jolly evenings provided inspiration during the deep night.

His latest book was a mystery set in her island village, a prospect both frightening and exciting. She was afraid to find out whether he had confined her and the kids to his printed page. His ravishing heroines generally drove sports cars at high speeds with wind rushing through their hair instead of high mileage station wagons. Still, she was thrilled to be some part of his inspiration.

Peter stepped out of the back door as she and the boys pulled into the driveway. "Hey Lou. Go put your feet up and read that book you left on the counter. I need these guys for a few minutes. I got a hankerin' for some spiced crab and I need some help if we are gonna get enough to satisfy this appetite I worked up sleeping all day. You guys get the nets out of the shed. I've got the chicken necks."

The day couldn't have ended more perfectly for any of them. Louise hated crabbing while the boys loved it, but were still too young to do it on their own. Her feet longed for an elevated position in the air-conditioned living room and the book begged to be finished.

The crabs were plentiful and tasty with the pasta and ratatouille. Peter had scrounged up the ingredients for pots du chocolade from her cupboards.

The boys stayed up for the crab feast and barely managed to finish the scrumptious dessert. With the boys asleep, she and Peter retired to the screened porch to catch the evening breeze off the ocean. As soon as Louise's feet were up her eyelids sank and she bade Peter goodnight.

For Peter it was midmorning. He brought his laptop onto the

porch and set it up on the glassed top table facing the ocean. The soft breeze coaxed the words out of his fingers. Occasionally he raised his eyes to the middle distance where a huge, round, full moon was rising directly in front of him. He was trying to write a beach swimming scene when the words began to slow. It had been a long time since he had actually been in the ocean and he knew why. He could have blamed it on his nighttime hours, but the real reason was a deep personal secret.

Deep down he was afraid of those creatures lurking underneath the ocean's surface. He had just read an article by an Indian woman entitled, "A Well Lived Life the Indian Way—Facing and Overcoming Your Fears." Maybe if he walked down and stuck his toes in the water he could arouse his senses enough to make the scene come to life. Perhaps he could even start to face and overcome this fear.

He stood up, stretched his arms and plodded back through the house. The clock on the VCR read twelve twenty. He closed the back door quietly and walked barefoot on the warm pavement to the beach path. The dunes parted and he stepped onto a vast empty beach. The record of the day's activities in the sand had been smoothed out by the breeze.

His big footprints marred the tiny ripples in the windswept sand as the fine sand sifted between his bare toes. The moon shone so bright that it turned the sky into a deep blue instead of black. The world consisted of thin black silhouettes against the back lit sky.

The black sea oats swayed in the breeze and the beach houses were dark monoliths. The reflection of the white orb in the ocean cut an ever widening path from the shore to infinity. Tiny ripples crossed the surface until the waves broke close to shore dumping out the moonlight and extinguishing it on the sand. The white path invited him. Like the yellow brick road, the path seemed to lead to a heavenly body. He felt like he could walk on the path across the water out to the moon.

He glanced to the right and the left and saw only beach for

miles and miles in each direction, gently curving to form an empty black crescent. He stood at the edge of the white highway exactly in the center of the crescent and breathed deeply several times to take in the warm heavy salt air. He might be the only person on earth. He stepped to the water's edge. In the wet sand beside his feet dots of phosphorus blinked off and on.

The wave's tongues licked his feet and the warm water begged him to come in. He hadn't brought a bathing suit but it seemed much better to swim in the buff under the protective moonlight. He stepped back from the water's edge into the wide expanse of sand and disrobed. Folding his clothes into a neat stack, he placed his baseball cap on top and noted that the pile of clothes seemed to be the only protrusion rising from the sand for miles in either direction.

Peter walked into the water at the very center of the white path. Feeling tall, virile and a little excited as he strode naked into the moonlit sea. He pushed himself through the tiny waves to bigger ones that broke against his thighs, sending grains of sand and tiny bits of shell against his bare legs. He passed the waves and lowered himself slowly into the salty warm ocean water and keeping faithfully to the center of the white light on the ocean's ripples, he swam out a long distance.

From nowhere the hideous shark scene from Jaws came into his head and he fleetingly wondered if his dangling appendage could possibly attract a shark. He forced those thoughts out of his head, rolled on his back and looked up into the twinkling heavens. After living in New York for so long he had begun to assume that most of the stars had gone out—at least all but the brightest ones. Not so here in the South, where the sky was crowded.

Lying on his back in the ocean, he felt calm as a sleeping baby; his arms floated straight out from his shoulders, while his legs arched down deeply below him. The water held him gently, like a lover, and wrapped its fingers warmly around the parts within its grasp. The moist air had a strangely sensual scent and he found himself running his hands down his own body until soon he was completely aroused.

A golden haired mermaid, straight out of a children's book his mother had read him long ago, surfaced beside him. Her eyes widened and she gave a hint of a smile at his condition. She was even more beautiful than he remembered with the moonlight highlighting the gold in her hair.

She put her hands admiringly on his chest and ran her fingers down to his thighs. She squeezed them lightly and then moved her hands toward the center. Peter was a bit frightened at the prospect of an alien creature touching him *there* but he found fear only aroused him more. She seemed genuinely curious at this protruding part. He felt her nipple brush his side.

Tentatively she ran the side of her finger up the shaft and tweaked the head gently with her nail. Then she put both index fingers at the base of the shaft and moved them quickly up anddown, back and forth. Suddenly she stopped and disappeared. Just as quickly her golden head bobbed up between his legs.

This time she was smiling and laughing as to Peter's horror she gently cupped his balls in her hands and gave them a little squeeze. She pulled her head up onto his belly and pushed her ample bosoms tight around his member. She moved her shoulders in a rotating motion as she tweaked her own nipples. This was it for Peter. She felt him coming and pushed his torso underwater just in time.

He jerked and twisted as his sperm pushed against the resistance of the seawater and the soft breast. When he finally stopped his spasmodic movement she disappeared. He lay there for a long time with his eyes closed savoring the moment while he rested and regained his strength.

He was furious with himself for never swimming at night before. Much later he rolled onto his stomach and began a slow even crawl towards the distant beach. It was much farther than he thought and he pulled himself exhausted onto the shore. The tide had risen and the beach had been reduced by half.

He nuzzled his bare bottom into the sand and laid back with his hands behind his head and stared into the twinkling ceiling. He let himself fly through space, his soul shooting then floating through the universe.

It had been a magical evening but he was tired and he began to wish for the soft pillow in Louise's guest room. He rolled his head to the right to sight down the beach for the protrusion that would be his clothes. Nothing. He turned his head to the left and did the same. Nothing.

A synapse in his brain delivered the answer. He hadn't reckoned on the tide. That mermaid was probably wearing his favorite baseball cap. Ah well, she deserved it.

Suddenly the world became darker as a cloud began to obscure the moon. Behind him the black silhouettes of the palm trees tickled the night sky.

He scanned the beach and saw nothing familiar. Worse yet, he didn't know whether to walk to the right or the left. After attempting to judge the current he tentatively walked to the right. Peter looked out to sea and saw that the white path had disappeared.

He turned to the shoreline and a shiver went up his spine as he realized the silhouettes had melted into the background to form a thick black jungle that came between him and civilization. It was the middle of the night and he was naked and completely lost in a wild area of the beach. The wind picked up and goose bumps started at his neck and spread quickly down his whole body.

He walked along the shore in the darkness looking for a path through the jungle. He finally found what looked like a passageway. Moving gingerly he edged forward one careful footstep at a time. He managed to put his foot into a patch of sand burrs, and he let out a scream as he jerked his foot back. He halted for a moment and contemplated his predicament. It was now so dark that he could not make out his own fingers down at the end of his arm. The wind had picked up and chilled his naked body.

He contemplated the solutions. He could wait here for Louise

322-MORT

to discover his absence and send out a search party. She might not discover his absence until evening so it might be a long wait. The way the mosquitoes were biting there might not be much of him left.

The only other option was to keep going and find the way home himself. He pressed forward, every step worse than the last. He trudged through a swampy area with squishy water up to his ankles. His skin was brushed, snagged and torn by the tropical vegetation.

Once he put his foot down and something cold and clammy slithered from underneath his foot. Up ahead he saw a break in the vegetation and to his horror came out again on the beach, having needlessly left pieces of his naked body on the thorns and bushes of a giant half circle.

He trudged down the beach looking for an opening in the tangle of underbrush. At last he saw a real path between the dunes and he timidly sought out the path in the darkness. After a long and tedious walk he looked up and shivered at the welcome sight of the dark monoliths, but the configuration of the monoliths was not the same as on Louise's path and he suddenly grew acutely aware of his nakedness.

He passed one of the windmill palm trees and cut his hand wrenching one of the smaller leaves off the tree to use as a shield for his private parts. He came out onto a road and into the headlights of a car. The car slowed but Peter slid back into the shadows with his protective palm leaf.

Peter trudged along the road until he found a house with a light on. He boldly knocked on the door. A shadow fell across the glass in the door and the door opened the length of a security chain.

The eyes peering out the little opening narrowed menacingly. "Who are you and what do you want? You're naked behind that palm leaf, aren't you? What kind of place do you think this is anyway? I'm calling the police."

The door slammed in his face and Peter took off running.

Halfway down the street he stubbed his toe and plunged head-long onto the asphalt severely damaging his palm leaf and bloodying his knees and palms. He picked himself up, brushed off and commenced running again for many blocks, going as fast as his limited physical condition would allow, turning left and right and ignoring the wear on his bare feet.

He came to a corner and fell exhausted onto a soft looking yard, rolled into the dark shadows cast by the landscaping and carefully covered himself with his torn palm leaf. To his horror a security light clicked on and illuminated the entire yard. As he lay still a moment a familiar flashing light caught his eye. The neon light of the all night pizza parlor. He was only two blocks from Louise's! He rolled to the edge of the yard, stood up and made his way home.

He quietly opened the door to Louise's house and stepped into the kitchen. Louise turned from the sink where she was getting a glass of water and he saw her eyes widen in horror. "Where have you been? What exactly do you do when I am asleep?"

WHEN MY DADDY LAY DYING[3]

When my daddy lay dying, my little boy Kenny, he wasn't but four-year old or so. I think he knew something bad was fixing to happen because of the way the grownups were acting. You know how people'll do when something like that's happening. They'll talk in whispers and tiptoe all around and make faces at the young'uns to get them to hush up.

Anyhow, Kenny, he asked me what was going on and I told him God was getting ready to come get Grandpa and take him on up to Heaven.

Well, Grandpa, he died early the next morning around eight o'clock.

About a half-hour later, Kenny was outside riding his tricycle when he seen this here big old black hearse come up in the drive-way and stop and this man in a dark navy blue suit get out. Kenny, he jumped off his trike and run up to the front door, just hollering.

"Mama! Mama!" he said. "God's here!"

—*Bert Goolsby*

WHITE LIES

Pamela Armstrong Stockwell

Adapted from her unpublished novel
Coming to Terms

So. Now you are angry because you have found out where you come from and it is different from what you've been told, no? I know. You feel like we have lied to you. Well, you are right. We did. But we did it because we thought it was the best thing. Yes, yes, we have always told you lying was bad. But sometimes, you want to protect the people you love and lying seems the best way to do it.

But now you are older. Perhaps now it is time. At any rate, it is the time to listen. If you want to be angry later, so be it.

We told you the truth about being from Germany, but we told you we came over long ago. This is not true. We lived in Germany during the war. We did not leave until after the war was over.

You see, before I met your father, I was married to someone else. And you are not my only child, as you have always thought. At the start of the problems, I was just in my mid-twenties. I was happily married to Isaac, a nice, considerate man. We had been married for seven years. We had two children, Sonia and Ira. We lived in a modest townhouse in Berlin, and Isaac ran a large and prosperous grocery. We were not wealthy, but we did, as they say here, pretty well.

I am starting at the time that we knew things were bad, 1936.

322-MORT

Before that, there was talk. Laws changed. Our rights were gradually taken away because we were Jewish. First one thing, than another. But because we were Jewish, we thought 'Ah, again. This, too, shall pass.' Because you see, this had happened for thousands of years, and we had survived. And this was the twentieth century. The modern era. Someone would put a stop to the madman Hitler. It was a passing thing, we thought. If only we had risen up in defiance of the laws. Would things have been different? Only God knows.

Some people were smarter than others. They saw the signs and left. We were slow. By the time we woke up, it was too late. Everyone had closed their doors. But I get ahead of myself.

Have you heard of Kristallnacht? No? It was the beginning of the bad time. The real beginning of the Holocaust that you have heard about. Before that, it was simply some laws. It was people being able to hate us openly, with looks and closed doors. After Kristallnacht, however. . . everything changed after that.

My mother had been sick. She was dying of the cancer and was in hospital. We were very tired. We had sat up with her night after night. This one night she seemed peaceful, so we went to bed early and slept soundly. Until the most awful crashing woke us up. Our hearts were pounding in our chests. Ah, you can't imagine! We thought we were being bombed, but it was the sound of glass breaking all over Berlin. Windows being smashed everywhere.

We went to the windows and looked out and saw the sky lit up. We found out later it was the synagogues burning. But though we didn't know this right then, we were afraid it was about us. All the trouble lately was about Jews. We gathered up Sonia and Ira and huddled in our hallway until dawn as the world crashed around us.

The next morning, we went out cautiously. Our feet crunched on the glass that looked like so much carpet on the sidewalks. We went to our store. It was destroyed. Years later, I almost laughed at how I cried then. How I thought my heart was breaking. What did I know about how much a heart can break?

They had destroyed everything. Everything. Canned goods, produce, registers, countertops, shelves. Nothing was left. Everything we had worked so hard for. What were we going to do? we wondered. Then, not knowing what else to do, we went to the hospital to make sure Mother was all right and not too frightened from all the rioting.

But the hospital had not escaped the terrible night. My mother was not there. They had forced all the patients out into the street, including my sick mother, who couldn't even hold a spoon up to feed herself. Frantic, we went from house to house around the hospital asking if anyone had seen her. We found her in one of those houses. A Christian family had taken her in, and she lay in their bed. Her feet were cut from the glass. The Nazis had made the patients walk barefoot out into the night. We carried her home and she died three days later, without ever regaining consciousness. She was a lucky one. She got out early.

After that, as I said, everything changed. My son, my little Ira, was beat up at school one day, and the boys who beat him painted a swastika on his clothes. He came home bleeding from his ears and nose. The German boys, some he used to play with, had kicked him in the head and spit on him, called him disease-carrying Jew. He cried and cried. He was only six. What did he know about what was going on?

They came one night and got Isaac. Just came, pounded on the door and took him away. He came back two weeks later, thin, so thin, and not himself anymore. He'd been interrogated about the underground. I never knew if he knew anything about it or not. I think he did, but he didn't tell me to protect me. But while he was being held, he was beaten. They strip-searched him. He was made to clean bathrooms that a decent human being wouldn't even want to go in. His cellmate hung himself in the middle of the night, and he didn't hear it. He awoke the next morning to see the man's body swinging from a beam, his face black. The guards made Isaac cut the man down and drag him out of the cell. The body was already stiff. This is all he told me. I think there was more that he couldn't say. Some things you just can't tell, not even your wife. He had terrible nightmares afterwards.

One day, I took Sonia with me to the bakery as I often did. She was only four. As we walked down the street, some boys—they were about twelve—began taunting us, calling us dirty Jews. They threw garbage at us. Sonia cried, turning to me for protection. What could I do? I could be arrested if I so much as raised my voice at the boys. I ducked my head and grabbed Sonia and we ran. I was so ashamed that I couldn't do more. Again, I thought my heart was breaking. I did not know it could go on breaking and breaking, like the glass of Kristallnacht. One heartache piled upon another.

We had to wear armbands so that everywhere we went, people could spit on us. Little Ira went one day to get us bread, and two men were standing at the door talking, one holding it open. He walked through, under the man's arm and the man hit him with a rolled-up newspaper. "I wasn't holding the door for you, you filthy Yid," the man said.

But these were small things. Before long, we had to give up the house. Some soldiers came and told us we had fifteen minutes to pack what we could. The rest would be confiscated. We packed our clothes, our family pictures. A violin. My jewelry we had already sewn into the hems of our clothes. We each had several pieces sewn into different garments, because we did not know what would happen. If we were separated, we would at least have something to sell.

We left our home as the soldiers watched. I remember one young man, he could not meet our eyes. He looked ashamed. I often thought of him over the years. He had decency. Did it get stamped out of him? Was he able to hang onto it? It seemed so few did.

We tried to get out of Germany, but like so many others, we had waited too long. All the other countries had closed their doors. England, Italy, Australia, Brazil, America. We tried them all. But no one would take us.

As the months passed, more and more Jews were rounded up and taken to work camps, but rumors came back of unspeakable things. Unbearable conditions, beatings and torture and mass shootings. We did not want to believe what we heard, but we knew the Nazis. Deep down, I think, we thought them capable of these evil things we heard about.

So we went into hiding. Gentile friends of ours took us in, kept us in their basement for over a year. There were no windows. We spent fourteen months in the dark, like rats. We would sometimes go upstairs at night to get fresh air, but that was all. Once every couple of months, we would go into the house during the day, just to see the light. This was a terrible risk, but we felt we would die for a glimpse of light.

One day, we heard a pounding at the door, a sound we had dreaded and that to this day will almost make my heart stop with a terrible fear. Moments later, we heard Franz, our friend, protesting that there was no one else in the house. We heard cries, then a shot. Then heavy booted feet thumped on the floor boards over our heads as the Nazis searched. Suddenly, the door to the basement was thrown open. Light poured in, blinding us, but not so much that we didn't see the silhouette of a Nazi soldier.

He forced us upstairs at gunpoint, poking us with his bayonet, drawing blood or not, he didn't care. Franz lay on the floor, a tiny red circle on his forehead and a pool of blood beneath his head. His eyes were open, staring up at a God who we thought had turned his face away. His wife, Inga, huddled in a corner, clutching their son and sobbing. I felt as if we had each shot Franz ourselves.

We were taken to a detention center and separated. Children here, women there, men over there. My children looked at me as they were led away, tears in their eyes, faces taut with fear. I wanted to reach for them, take them away. I raised an arm without thinking, and a soldier slammed it down with the butt of his rifle. He broke my arm, but I hardly noticed the pain as I saw Sonia mouth the word "Mommy." That was the last I ever saw of my children.

I was taken to Mauthausen. There I remained until the Americans came and liberated us. It was several years, I think. I lost all track of time. When I was released, I weighed less than ninety pounds. Many people I had gotten to know died. Some of dysentery, some of other typhus or other diseases. Some were shot. Some were gassed. There were so many ways to die. I don't know why I lived.

After the war, as soon as I had enough strength, I began to search for my family. According to records, my husband was sent to Buchenwald where he died of dysentery near the end of the war. My children were sent to the gas chambers almost as soon as they arrived at Dachau. All those years that I prayed to God to keep them safe, and He already had them with Him. If I had known, I am sure I too would have died. It was the thought of them that gave me strength to fight for a crust of bread. To wake up and face the filth of the latrines. To watch people wasting away around me.

So there I was, the war over, and I was alive and alone. Breathing, not really living. I don't know how I lived through the next few years. All I know is the sun kept coming up everyday, in spite of everything. I got up, I ate, I slept again.

One day, I was able to remember Sonia and Ira and Isaac with a smile instead of always the tears. I came to America, met Josef Birnbaum, and we married. He had been from Poland. I could never have married someone who did not know what it had been like. There is too much in my head and too much in my heart. God blessed me with you. He gave me a second family.

At first, I didn't intentionally keep from you all I have just told you. But at what point do you tell a child such horrors? How could I let my nightmares haunt your own dark nights? No, it isn't right that you should be kept in ignorance of your brother and sister, but day by day, we got on with the business of living. Now you notice the tattoo on my arm, and you ask. If you are old enough to ask, I guess you are old enough to know.

Ah, you are not angry anymore? You feel sad for your lost relatives. Oh, for my suffering? No, no. You must not feel sad for me. I still have times when I am angry, and I ask God why, but He tells me, Frieda, life is a gift. And I say why then did You take it from so many? And He says, you think I did that? He says when Franz saved you, that was Me. When the Christians took your mother in, that was Me. When you met Josef and had another child, that was Me. But I can only work when allowed to work and your anger is not allowing Me to work.

So you see, little one, I have learned to listen to God. Sometimes, anyway. Forgive me my lies, but know that I did what I thought was best. I wanted you to grow up happy and secure, one step away from the terrible time your father and I went through. And look at you! Bursting with good health and doing so well. Your eyes have never seen hate and destruction and death. This is my wish for you—that you never do.

322-MORT

EVER THOUGHT OF SELF-PUBLISHING?

C. Tolbert Goolsby, Jr.

Tell me, friend, have you written a book that's lying around, going no place, and not being read? Have rejection slips got you down? Do you sincerely believe the book nonetheless has merit and people would purchase it if only the book was for sale in bookstores? Is that what's bothering you, friend?

Cheer up. Consider self-publishing.

Have you ever read Pat Conroy's book *The Boo*? It was his first book. Conroy self-published it. Conroy, as you know, went on to write, among other works, *Prince of Tides*, *The Great Santini*, *The Water is Wide*, *The Lords of Discipline*, and *Beach Music*.

What about *The Christmas Box*? Ever heard of that? Its author first published the story for his family and friends and ran only a few copies. Somehow, people found out about the book and began asking for it in the bookstores. Later, a publisher discovered it. The rest, as they say, is history.

You could do the same thing. It's not as difficult to do as you might think, but it will cost you some money up front. That's why you must believe sincerely your book has merit and people will buy it.

Select a Book Manufacturer

How to begin? The first thing to do is to select a book manufacturer (note the use of the word "manufacturer," not "publisher"). Most good size communities have one or more book manufacturers; but if your town does not have one, don't worry. There are plenty elsewhere.

Whether you use a local or foreign book manufacturer, you need to determine from the manufacturer what its requirements are. Most are able to take good quality typewritten or computer-generated text prepared by you and manufacture your book directly from it. Some are not so equipped or prefer to manufacture your book using a different method.

You may obtain names and addresses of book manufacturers by using the yellow pages or looking at advertisements in books or magazines such as the *Writer's Digest*. Simply write a brief letter to the manufacturer or, if it has one, dial its 800 number. Most respond very promptly. Some will send you examples of their work along with their guidelines, particularly if you have some idea about how you want you book to be done.

Here are a couple of examples:

(1) Morris Publishing in Kearney, Nebraska. One thing I like about this company is the publishing guide it sends that explains everything you need to know from preparation of the manuscript to copyrights and bar codes. The guide, which is in booklet form, is really a good resource tool for self-publishing.

(2) Adams Press in Chicago. I used it for my first book, *Sweet Potato Biscuits and Other Stories*. Its brochure provides a price list and explains all that it can do for you, including copyright service and other services.

(3) Wentworth Publishing in Columbia, South Carolina, a local publisher. I used it for my second book, *The Box With the Green Bow and Ribbon*.

322-MORT

Should you use a foreign or local book manufacturer? Using the foreign manufacturer may prove less expensive - provided no problems emerge.

The advantage of using a local book manufacturer is that you can discuss problems face to face. You don't incur long distance charges (if the company does not have an 800 or 888 number), which can add to the costs of your book, and you don't have to spend large amounts of time writing and drafting correspondence. In addition, you save on shipping and handling. In short, it's easier and less complicated to deal with local people; and many local manufacturers are equipped to provide you just as good a service as those elsewhere.

Preparation of the Manuscript

After you have selected a book manufacturer, you must prepare your manuscript in accordance with its requirements. Most manufacturers will have an outline, brochure or booklet explaining what you are to do. Again, Morris uses a booklet while Adams uses a brochure.

How you prepare your manuscript depends on what process you will use to reproduce your book. You must choose between regular "typeset printing," and "offset printing"?

"Typeset printing" means that type is set from your manuscript.

Both books I have self-published used "offset printing." A manufacturer using this process takes each page of your manuscript - the hardcopy - and photographs it. The negatives then are used in the printing process. If you select this process to manufacture your book, you must provide the manufacturer pages that are "camera ready," *i.e.,* ready for the camera. This is the most economical method for the printing of books.

As with any process, offset printing has advantages and disadvantages. A major disadvantage is that the negative pretty much locks in stone your pagination. For instance, if when you are proof-reading a "bluelined copy," *i.e.,* a proof, and you discover an error on, let's say, page 120 and the book is 200 pages long, chances are any correction on page 120 will affect all the pages that follow. If it does so, you have a major problem. Each page might have to be rephotographed or reset and you must pay for that, increasing your costs.

Still the offset process is rather simple and comparatively inex-pensive, at least up until the pages are actually photographed and later on as well, provided you can avoid making mistakes in pre-paring the original for duplication.

If you select the offset method, you must, therefore, carefully prepare your manuscript to make it camera ready. The printing you do at home forms the foundation for all that follows. The manuscript must be neat, complete, and correct. It must also meet the manufacturer's requirements as to size and clarity.

What you see on the manuscript that you deliver to the manu-facturer is exactly what you will get back because it is essentially a photograph of what you gave to the manufacturer. If there is a smudge on page 4, there will be a smudge on page 4 of the fin-ished product; if a word is misspelled on the manuscript, it will be misspelled on the finished product. So edit and proofread your manuscript very carefully before you submit it to the manufac-turer.

Regarding size, this can be pretty much what you and the manufacturer agree upon. My book *The Box With the Green Bow and Ribbon* measures, for example, 4.25 inches by 5.50 inches.

Regarding the clarity, your printer ought to have at least 600 dpi (dots per inch) clarity.

What about the fonts you use? This is your choice, of course. You will probably want to select two or more. One for the text and another for the headers or footers. A good choice for the text, and the one that I used for both my books, is "Times New Roman."

And art work? Again, this is something you need to discuss with the particular manufacturer. Some employ their own graphic artists while others don't. Whether the manufacturer does so or not will not matter. It will be able to reproduce what you provide it and will be able to discuss with you the question of inks and colors. The manufacturer will provide you with swatches to help you decide on what colors you want.

Another thing you will discuss with the manufacturer is the weight of the paper to be used. Usually, you should select a paper of between 50 and 80 lb. weight. You don't want to use paper that the ink might bleed through. If you have a book with a small number of pages, you might want to use a thicker paper. A thicker paper will make the book appear thicker.

At this point, there are two other questions you need to answer before your book can become a reality. Is your book to be "case bound" or "perfect bound", hardback or softback? Case bound means the pages of the book are sewn together and is in hardback while perfect bound means the pages of the book are glued together. Obviously, the case bound is more expensive.

Some other questions you will need to answer at this point are (1) whether you want to secure a registered copyright for your book; (2) do want an ISBN number and bar code on your book; and (3) do you want to obtain a Library of Congress number. Some book manufacturers provide this service for your but at a cost. The process for obtaining these items is not difficult and you can save some money here by doing it yourself.

For a copyright registration, write and obtain forms from the Register of Copyrights, Copyright Office, Library of Congress, Washington, D.C. 20559-6000. Complete the application form AFTER YOU HAVE GOTTEN YOUR BOOKS PUBLISHED and enclose a $20 check and two copies of the book.

You may want to obtain a Library of Congress number. The book must be at least 50 or more pages to qualify for its catalog. You have to provide the library with a nonrefundable copy of the book upon publication. The application must be submitted BEFORE PUBLICATION of the book. The number must be printed on the copyright page, which is the reverse side of the title page and it must be preceded by the words, "Library of Congress Catalog Number." The application is simple and can be obtained by writing to Library of Congress, Cataloging in Publication Division, 101 Independence Avenue, S.E., Washington, D.C. 20540-4320. It will send you a booklet entitled *PCN Publishers Manual Guidelines for the Preassigned Card Number Program.*

If you plan to use an ISBN number, you must obtain this number BEFORE you can file for the Library of Congress number. To obtain a form to secure an ISBN number, contact ISBN U.S. Agency, R.R. Bowker, 121 Chalon Rd., New Providence, NJ 07974. Complete the form and return it to the same address along with a check for $165 or if you want faster service, for $215. R.R. Bowker will then send you a block of numbers to be used, ten in all. The printer will use one of these numbers and craft you a bar code. The ISBN number will appear on the copyright page inside your book.

A final question you need to answer: How many books do you want to print? The more you order the less the book costs per unit. The question of how many books to print is a very difficult question to answer. Included in it are the questions of your ability to pay and how much you can afford to lose financially; your ability to market or effectively promote your book; who your market really is, including distributors and retail vendors; and whether these markets will distribute, sell, or buy your book. The question of whether people will buy your book depends in large measure on how much it will cost and how much it will cost will determine how much it will sell for. And when you think about how much a book is to sell for, remember this - think wholesale not retail - even less than wholesale, if you are to use a book distributor.

In answering the question of how many books to manufacture, you also need to consider this question? What do you expect to gain from the investment? What you can expect to gain are these things: (1) a publishing history that you can refer to in all your correspondence with book publishers; (2) a sample you can send to book publishers later on, especially if the book is moder-

)322-MORT

ately successful; (3) a legacy for your children and grandchildren irrespective of whether it earns a dime; (4) a gift you can send to friends and relations - your parents will appreciate it and your mother-in-law will be absolutely stunned. Say what you will, a published book, whether you do it or someone else does it, gives you a history of publication. For writers, that is important.

One more thing about the manufacturing process: give yourself plenty of lead time. This process itself takes time and you are bound to encounter delays and problems you didn't anticipate. So, for example, if you are planning to publish a Christmas book, start the publication process no later than July 1.

Marketing the Book

What I have learned about marketing I learned by trial and error. I have self-published two books and what follows is derived entirely from those two experiences.

Where should you begin the marketing process? Begin at home. Recruit your spouse, your parents, your brothers and sisters, your in-laws, and your friends to help you find markets - bookstores that will handle self-published books.

How to find the book stores? Simple. You look in the yellow pages. After making a list of the bookstores, visit each one and asked for the manager or other person who is in charge of purchasing. Have a book with you to show the manager and be prepared to leave it with the manager, if necessary. If you have a synopsis of the book or other write up, give that to the manager as well.

Most of the stores I have dealt with, big or small, will purchase a regional or local book that a person has self-published for its regional or local bookshelf. Usually, they will take the book on consignment. This means that if the book retails for $10.00, a bookstore will pay you 40 per cent less for the book, or $6.00.

If you are going to distribute your own book, two things you need are a ledger book and a billing or invoice pad. You can buy these items at most office supply stores or stores that carry office

supplies. As any salesperson would do when a store buys a product, you would give the store a bill or invoice reflecting the amount due and owing, the number of books delivered, the date of delivery, and the name of the vendor. You would keep a copy of the invoice. Always make sure someone in the store signs both copies of the invoice to acknowledge delivery of the books.

When you get home, you would record the transaction in a ledger book under an entry or topic called vendor sales. In your ledger book, you would also keep track of expenses, consignments, gifts, private retail sales, defective books returned to the manufacturer for a refund or adjustment, and books used for promotional purposes, along with expenses incurred.

Speaking of bookstores, there are all types: the big chains; the newsstands; the mom and pop operations; and college bookstores. Don't forget your alma mater. Each college I have attended has a bookstore and each of those stores has an "Alumni and Faculty" shelf within the store.

Some outlets, particularly the large chains, will not buy directly from the author. How do you get into those stores? You do this by contacting a book distributor. Most large towns have at least one. If not, just visit a bookstore and ask the manager who distributes books to the store. Some stores will have several distributors. Get these names and addresses, and either call or write the distributor and tell the distributor about your book. Most distributors will charge you 15 per cent to distribute your book, with the distributor paying the costs of distribution and of collection of amounts due. Note that the profit margin shrinks if you use a book distributor. Instead of getting 60 per cent back on the sale of a book at retail, you will get only 45 per cent. You need to be aware of this when deciding the question of the number of books you will manufacture.

There is another market besides book stores for your book. This market is called "the back door market": your friends, your associates at work, your neighbors, and your relatives. Don't count very much on the latter - your mama, maybe. For some reason,

322-MORT

relatives feel they should be given the book. Many of your friends will feel the very same way.

What you can do with this market is cut them a deal. You sell the book at less cost than the bookstores would sell the book for but for more than the book cost you to manufacture. But this approach has a draw back. It undercuts your vendors. Nonetheless, sell what you can when you can. After all, it's your money that's been invested in the manufacture of the book. People who offer to buy a book directly from you might not want to take the trouble of going down to the bookstore.

Still you might want to encourage them to buy from your book vendors - particularly when you will be at a store to do a book signing. There are few things more humiliating than sitting behind a table in a bookstore ready to sign books and the only person who stops wants to know where the rest room is.

Promotion

How to promote your book? Again, I'm no expert but this is what I have done.

When contacting the bookstores in the first instance, offer to do a book signing for them at a mutually convenient time and place. Some bookstores advertise in the local press about upcoming book signing events in their stores. The more your book is written about, the more likely people are going to learn about it. You will find most bookstores are anxious to have authors come into their stores and autograph their books.

Contact your local newspaper and see if it will run an article about your book. Some papers will assign a local reporter to do a story about you and your book. Other papers may want "canned" material. For instance, I had an author friend do a book review. He sent the review to a newspaper and it published the review. So, he benefited by having a review published, I benefited by having a review of my book published, and the paper had space filled. Most importantly, the newspaper's readers learned of my book.

Be prepared to do a lot of your own promotion even when you are slated to do a book signing.

You should contact local radio and television stations and ask to appear on their talk shows. Each time I've been on a radio talk show or made a television appearance, sales of the book have shot up momentarily.

Participate, if given the opportunity, in book fairs and writer workshops.

Send a notice off to your alumni magazine that you've published a book and tell readers how they may contact you and purchase it.

My wife and I one time even rented a booth at a flea market.

Just use your imagination. Include a notice about your book in your church bulletin; don't be hesitant to talk about your book; offer to speak to civic clubs about the book, conditioned on your being able to sell the book "back door" style after the speech.

Another fruitful source of publicity: use the book as gifts to friends, relatives, and yes - even donate them to be used to raise money for others, *e.g.*, telethons and other charitable activities.

Regarding marketing, you should also think about how to display your book, even if it is to be placed on a shelf with other books. My wife came up with an idea of using small, gold-colored boxes to which she affixed some green ribbon and a bow in which to display my book *The Box With the Green Bow and Ribbon*. The box keeps the books separate from others and keeps them from getting scattered. We usually ask the retailer to place the box next to the cash register or on a table with other Christmas stories.

Licenses

Finally, I should mention this matter. We all work for the government in the United States—one way or the other.

License requirements are not the same everywhere. Before you begin the marketing of your book, you should determine whether your city and county require permits or licenses of any kind. In

South Carolina, for example, I had to get a permit from the county to operate a business from my home; I had to purchase a retail license permit from the state; I have to make periodic reports on sales and use taxes I collect and transmit those taxes to the state; and I have to include the amounts earned on my state and federal income tax forms.

With regard to sales and use taxes, and again depending on where you live, you may have to get a signed, written statement from each retailer that the retailer will be responsible for the collection of those taxes from purchasers. We must do that in South Carolina.

Regarding taxes, be careful to keep receipts of all expenses. These expenses include but are not limited to the following: (1) cost of publication; (2) cost of artwork; (3) cost of long-distance telephone calls; (4) cost of distribution or transportation; (5) cost of publicity.

Conclusion

The book that you have written can be printed and sold. You can do yourself. But it takes money, patience, imagination, and effort. A lot of the latter. The publishing process is not difficult at all. In fact, that's the easy part. The marketing process is more difficult and requires effort and imagination and adherence to government licensing requirements.

The payoff? A publishing history, a legacy, and the thrill of seeing your work in print and actually holding it in your hands!

GROUP THERAPY: MEET THE INKPLOTS

Writing in a vacuum was, at least for me, not very productive. Looking for guidance, I joined a fiction writing class at a local technical college. I came away from the class with much more than I anticipated—a solid core of people who shared my dream of writing.

At the end of the class, some of us created our own group, which became a sounding board for our writing. We were all searching for structure to channel our creative flow and constructive criticism to help us become better writers. Many of us wrote nonfiction in our jobs, but none of us were fiction writers.

Our different backgrounds provide a wide range of knowledge and insight. A judge, a lawyer, two therapists, a police detective, a public relations specialist, a lobbyist, a stay-at-home mother, a university administrator, an artist and a retired person comprise the Ink Plots. We have diversity in age, sex, religion and politics. This diversity makes for lively and intense meetings. How convenient it is to show up with a question and have it answered by an experienced member. We help each other through writer's block, catch each other's mistakes, correct grammatical errors, discuss plot and story lines and commiserate over deaths and divorces. A writing group, we have found, is an intimate endeavor.

We discuss the business end of writing. How do you get an agent? How does one write an effective synopsis? What books should we be reading? What conferences would be good to attend? As a result of our culling and sharing, we grow.

Our group, The Inkplots, assembles at seven each Tuesday. After chatting and catching up, we get a show of hands as to who brought something to read that week. One person passes out copies of his or her work to the others. Either the person reads his work aloud or the person asks someone else to read it and each member edits the piece as it is being read. Discussion and suggestions follow. We pass the copies back to the author with our suggestions and editing, but the author is then free to accept or ignore our insights.

How can you start a group like mine?

1. Look for members. From our experience, there are many writers out there. We found each other in a college short course. You might post a notice on a college or library bulletin board, run an ad in the paper, check with your local library or book store, or surf the net. Talk with your state arts commission about writer's workshops. It will take a while for your group to gel. Reading to others and being open to their criticism is very intimidating. Those who are not really committed or who can't take the criticism may silently slip away.

2. Be dedicated. Meet on a regular basis and be prompt. It is easy to let writing get lost in life's shuffle. We meet once a week and have for four years as we believe that it keeps us going forward at a good clip with our writing. If you don't have something to read every week, come to the meeting anyway, as you will find that you will learn a great deal about your own writing from helping others with esoteric points of grammar and plot.

3. Once your group has gelled, add new members carefully. Welcome visitors so they can see how your group works, but add new members only if the group approves.

4. Limit the number in your group. We now have eleven and that is a good number.
5. Apportion the time somewhat equally. We have occasionally used stopwatch to more equally apportion the two hours in our meeting.

6. Location and atmosphere are important. We tried meeting in a coffeehouse but now we meet in each other's homes and offices. We work best seated around a conference or dining room table. Take turns bringing refreshments.

7. No first drafts. Bring work that is polished. Don't waste everyone's time with grammatical or spelling errors.

8. Each writer should provide a typed copy of his or her work for each member. Feedback can be jotted down and kept by the author for future reference.

9. Make a list of everyone's address, telephone number, and e-mail address. Easy communication can hold a group together. Since we move around each week we have an active network of e-mails and phone calls.

10. Try doing a group exercise occasionally. We once wrote a progressive story that was passed around from week to week.

Over the past four years our group has written thousands of pages of fiction and completed six novels. One of our members has sold a novel for publication. This year we are publishing this compilation of some of our work. Working together we have accomplished things we could never have done individually. We bask in our collective success.

0322-MORT

AUTHORS' BIOGRAPHIES

John Bolin holds a bachelor's degree from Carson-Newman College and a masters degree in Education from the University of South Carolina. He spent two years as a public school teacher in Titusville, Florida, and two years as Registrar at North Greenville Junior College.

John is a career employee at the University of South Carolina having served ten years as Director, Undergraduate Admissions, five years as Associate Vice President for Administration, and fifteen years as Director, Carolina Coliseum. John is also an Adjunct Professor in the colleges of Applied Professional Sciences and Sports Administration.

For John, writing is spiritual, therapeutic, and entertaining.

Carla Damron, born in Sumter, SC, now resides in Columbia where she works as a clinical social worker. She developed a love for mysteries at about age eight and has been an avid reader ever since. She has completed two mystery novels and has a third in the works. In her mystery works and short stories, she uses her seventeen years experience as a therapist to explore the hidden motivations in her characters.

Carla is recently learned that her latest novel, *Adam's Fall*, has been accepted for publication in 2001.

Ann Furr grew up among the mountains of East Tennessee, although she has lived in the flat lands of South Carolina for thirty years. She was a teacher, a lawyer and a Judge. Except for a little teaching, she is now retired. She likes to travel, walk long distances and try new things. She has one perfect daughter, Shannon.

322-MORT

C. Tolbert Goolsby, Jr., grew up in Dothan, Alabama, and now lives in Columbia, South Carolina, with his wife Prue. He earned an undergraduate degree from The Citadel, a law degree from the University of South Carolina, and an advanced law degree from the University of Virginia. He is a former Chief Deputy Attorney General of South Carolina. He is the author of a nonfiction work, *The South Carolina Tort Claims Act: A Primer and Then Some* published by the South Carolina Bar. He is also the author of two recent works of fiction, *Sweet Potato Biscuits and Other Stories*, a collection of short stories, and *The Box With the Green Bow and Ribbon,* a Christmas short story. His fiction has appeared in *Back Porch* and in *St. Anthony Messenger.*

Judy Hubbard is a professional artist who has exhibited her work for over twenty years. Her multi-layered mixed media constructions utilize found objects, time-worn surfaces and transparent images to interpret and refract concepts relating to time. The creative process and the stories within these artworks have led Hubbard to writing.

Judy lives in Columbia, South Carolina, in an old house and works in its barn-turned-studio at the back of the rambling old garden. She is the wife of a law professor, the mother of two sons and the daughter and double granddaughter of Baptist preachers. This is the first publication of her writings.

Frances Jones attended Queens College, and in the 1950s, opened her own photo engraving shop. At the time, she was the only woman in the nation to head such a business. At one point she processed all but two of South Carolina's newspapers for the reading public.

She is past president of the Toastmistress Club and three-time past president of the Business and Professional Women's Club. Many of her short stories have been published in local newspapers. Frances has two children and several grandchildren who give her a lot of pleasure. She attributes her success to following this motto: "Work like you didn't intend to pray, and pray like you didn't intend to work."

Jeff Koob was born in Tokyo and grew up an Army brat. Although he has lived in the Southeast most of his life, he has lived abroad for almost ten years in Austria, Germany, and Jamaica. He has served in both the Army and the Peace Corps. With a BA in English from The Citadel and an MA in Psychology from West Georgia College, he has worked for more than twenty years as a psychotherapist. Jeff has written a novel and many short stories. He is married to Maria Madeo.

Righton H. McCallum, a graduate of Converse College, is a published poet and is a librarian. She lives in Summerville, South Carolina, with her husband Brown. They have two sons, one a student at the University of South Carolina School of Medicine and the other a student at Wofford College.

Sam Morton, author of *Uneasy Lies the Head* and *The Swingin' Neckbreaker*, is a 1985 graduate of The Citadel holding a bachelor's degree in English. He is a former detective supervisor and homicide investigator with the Richland County Sheriff's Office in Columbia, South Carolina. He is also a former professional wrestler.

Sam began his professional writing career in 1994 as a freelance writer. He served as an associate editor for *Greater Columbia Business Monthly* and *Florence Business Journal* magazines. He currently is a writer in the corporate communications department of a worldwide insurance and financial services software company. Maintaining his freelance work, Sam's articles regularly appear in *Columbia Metropolitan* and he is a contributing writer for *Lake Murray Magazine, Living in South Carolina*, and *Palmetto Professional*.

Pamela Armstrong Stockwell. A founding member of the Ink Plots, Pamela Armstrong Stockwell has worked in communications and advertising for over 10 years. She wrote her first

0322-MORT

short story when she was eight years old, but only in recent years has she become really interested in getting published. Her nearly completed novel, *Coming to Terms*, chronicles a family struggling to overcome the cycle of abuse and alcoholism.

Pamela also enjoys writing short stories and poetry. She teaches fiction writing, writes freelance and volunteers for the Rape Crisis Network. She holds a bachelor's degree in journalism from the University of South Carolina and currently works as a writer and strategist for a South Carolina power company. She lives in Columbia with her husband, Rich.

ENDNOTES

[1] With much thanks to Ellison D. Smith, IV.

[2] This story previously appeared in *Sweet Potato Biscuits and Other Stories* by the author and also in the December 1997 edition of *Back Porch* magazine.

[3] With much thanks to Pamela Stockwell. This short, short story is included in *Humanity, Darling,* a collection of short stories— a work in progress.

0322-MORT